HEALTHY
SEX

Dr. Miriam Stoppard

HEALTHY
SEX

DK PUBLISHING, INC.

A DK PUBLISHING BOOK

DESIGN & EDITORIAL Mason Linklater

SENIOR MANAGING ART EDITOR Lynne Brown
MANAGING EDITOR Jemima Dunne

SENIOR ART EDITOR Karen Ward
SENIOR EDITOR Penny Warren
US EDITOR Jill Hamilton

PRODUCTION Antony Heller

First American Edition, 1998
2 4 6 8 10 9 7 5 3 1

Published in the United States by
DK Publishing, Inc., 95 Madison Avenue,
New York, New York 10016

Visit us on the World Wide Web at http://www.dk.com

Library of Congress Cataloging-in-Publication Data

Stoppard, Miriam.
    Healthy sex / by Miriam Stoppard.
    p. cm. -- (DK healthcare series)
    Includes index.
    ISBN 0-7894-3093-2
    1. Sex instruction. 2. Sexual excitement. I. Title II. Series.
HQ56.S827   1998
613.9'.6--dc21   97-48493
                                                                CIP

Reproduced by Colourscan, Singapore
and IGS, Radstock, Avon
Printed in Hong Kong by Wing King Tong

CONTENTS

INTRODUCTION

Sex expresses something that nothing else can, and it is the main way that human beings show their love for each other. It has a place in your life that is as much as, or more important than, any other aspect of your relationships, be they long or short term. Beyond desire and procreation, sex is the time, place, means, and language of knowing someone else on a level different from all others.

At the heart of sex is also the importance men and women hold for each other, something that many people have lost sight of. Loving partners give the kind of support that no one else can; very often they are the only havens in the storms of life. They provide emotional backup; they help you to feel worthwhile, useful, and desirable. A loving partner makes you recognize yourself as a well-rounded and mature individual with every chance of happiness, and every right to it. And in this context, sex is of prime importance, because only a loving partner can give it. It is, therefore, the responsibility of every partner to do it well because, in the end, it is the one way of ensuring that a beloved companion will stay, and a loving relationship – with all its rewards – will endure.

But having a good sex life is not about sexual athletics, physical prowess, or just learning a series of sexual skills. This is why many sex manuals simply don't work; they emphasize the technical skills related to sexuality instead of the people involved. Experimenting with different techniques and positions doesn't guarantee to make you a better or more sophisticated lover. Good lovers are aware of the importance of closeness and caring; they desire to give love, to give pleasure, and to give themselves completely to their partners. The best lovers discover their partners' preferences through sharing the intimacy of mutual trust. The best sex is attained only in a truly loving, stable relationship that is nurtured, pursued, and withstands the test of time.

CHAPTER 1

THE TWO SEXES

Many men and women are successful, contented, and fulfilled in their voyages of sexual discovery. They're helped by sympathetic, caring partners who are open about their sexual needs and desires, who are prepared to initiate and experiment, and who understand their bodies and feel comfortable with their own sexuality.

For many others, however, sex is still a matter of just "doing it"; they've never known, or have forgotten, the considerable joys of giving and receiving love.

Practical information about male and female sexual anatomy and how it works can help rescue people from ignorance about sex, setting their sexual experiences on the road to becoming the ultimate expression of intimacy.

SEXUAL DEVELOPMENT

Both scientific research and personal observation have convinced me that men and women are more anatomically similar than are the males and females of most other species. Any two men or two women are likely to differ more in stature, size, and shape than does the average couple. The main differences between any two partners are their reproductive organs and the developmental changes apparent in their mature shapes that are caused by sex hormones.

⎯⎯ BOY INTO MAN ⎯⎯

The changes that mark a boy's physical development into a mature man begin in the preteen and early teen years and are completed when he is between 14 and 18. These changes – when boys become taller and more muscular, with wider shoulders, more developed genital organs, and with hair appearing on their genitals, underarms, faces, chests, arms, and legs – are caused mainly by the male hormone, testosterone. In addition to these changes, the adult male has experienced his voice "breaking" due to the larynx enlarging and the vocal cords becoming longer and thicker, which cause the pitch of the voice to drop. The activity of the sweat and sebaceous glands also increases during these years.

After testicular activity is established at puberty it normally continues for the rest of life with only slight impairment in later years. In old age there is a slight reduction in the production of sperm and androgen. This is associated with some degenerative changes in the testes, but there is no abrupt testicular decline comparable to the female climacteric.

The "average" man is approximately 5 feet 9 inches (173 centimeters) tall and weighs 162 pounds (74 kg); his chest, waist, and hip measurements are 39, 32, 37 inches (98, 80, 93 centimeters).

⎯⎯ GIRL INTO WOMAN ⎯⎯

In the latter part of adolescence, usually well after menstruation has begun, a girl's body begins to take on its female shape. (Prior to puberty, girls and boys, except for their external genitalia, are very similar.) The changes that a girl experiences are directly related to the secretion of female hormones, estrogen and progesterone. She gets taller, her hips and thighs get fleshier, and her figure is more rounded and curved. Her breasts begin to swell and hair grows under her arms and between her legs. Her internal and external genital organs grow and develop, and the vaginal wall starts to thicken. Vaginal secretions may appear.

A woman's ultimate shape is dependent on two things: the amount of hormones she produces, and the sensitivity of her body in reacting to these hormones.

At about the age of 45, ovarian function gradually wanes, and levels of estrogen and progesterone decline, resulting in cessation of menstruation and the loss of fertility, the thinning of the vaginal walls, and, very often, bone changes that result in a loss of height.

The "average" mature woman is 5 feet 3½ inches (158 centimeters) tall and weighs 135 pounds (61 kg); her bust, waist, and hip measurements are 36, 30, 38 inches (90, 75, 95 centimeters).

A MAN'S BODY

Skeleton Beginning at about age two, boys grow about 2 inches (5 centimeters) per year until the age of 13 or 14, when the sex organs begin to develop. Adolescence brings with it a rapid gain in both height and strength. The growth spurt that accompanies puberty may last for a few years, and during that time most boys gain approximately 3½ inches (9 centimeters) per year. At the end of this period of growth, the bones have grown harder, more brittle, and have changed in proportion. Once the shoulders broaden, the hips look narrower by comparison – a characteristic of the adult male.

Body hair Early in puberty, pubic hair appears at the base of the penis, and a while later, it starts growing on the scrotum as well. It may also grow around the anal area. Pubic hair normally grows in an upside-down triangle on the lower belly, although it may reach to the navel, and may grow outward toward the thighs. About one or two years later, hair will appear in the armpits and on the upper lip. Pubic hair is longer, coarser, and curlier than hair that has been on the body since birth. It may be a lighter or darker color than that on the head. As you grow older, it may turn gray.

In addition to curly pubic hair, hair appears on the arms, thighs, and lower legs. Hair may appear also on the chest, shoulders, and back, and the back of the hands. Facial hair becomes thicker and darkens as a man matures. The beard and moustache may be the same color as the hair on the head, or different.

The amount of body hair depends on racial or ethnic background and family history. Caucasian men generally have more body hair than oriental or black men; and "hairiness" runs in families.

A WOMAN'S BODY

Skeleton Starting at about age two, a girl grows at the average rate of 2 inches (5 centimeters) per year. Near the age of ten, she experiences a growth spurt and begins to grow at a faster rate, gaining approximately 4 inches (10 centimeters) or more in a single year, but then slows down again until she reaches her final height, approximately one to three years after the onset of menstruation. Although her bones are growing longer, not all of them grow at the same rate. Arm, leg, and feet bones grow at a faster rate than vertebrae, for instance, and the pelvic bones take on a characteristically wide shape.

A woman has a wider pelvis than a man, in order to accommodate a growing baby, and her thigh bones are set wider apart. The thighs have to slant quite steeply inward for the knees to come near the center of gravity, so most women have a degree of knock-knees.

Body hair Sexual body hair usually appears around the eleventh or twelfth year, just after the breasts have begun to grow. Pubic hair is longer, coarser, darker in color, and curlier than one's normal childhood hair, which has been present on the body since birth. Pubic hair first appears on the vulva and slowly spreads over the mons and vaginal lips, forming an upside-down triangle. In some women, pubic hair grows up toward the navel and out onto the thighs. Hair starts growing in the armpits almost two years after the appearance of pubic hair.

Women differ in how much pubic hair grows. Some have a great deal; for others it is sparse. Pubic hair can be any color and does not have to match the head hair. As a woman grows older, her pubic hair may turn gray.

A MAN'S BODY

Muscles The thighs, calves, shoulders, and upper arms begin to grow broader during adolescence, and strength increases, too. A grown man's muscles are 40 times those at birth. The main determinant of body strength is body size, and muscle itself accounts for 40 percent of total body weight.

The genitals The testes grow very slowly until about the age of 10 or 11, following which there is a considerable acceleration in growth of the external genital organs. In the fully grown male, the testes are usually about 1½ inches (3.8 centimeters) long, between ½ and 1 fluid ounce (16–27 milliliters) in volume, and are dusky colored. One testis, usually the left one, hangs lower than the other, so that they do not become crushed against each other when you walk. In most men, testes are the same size, but in a few, one may be larger than the other.

Changes to the penis begin at a later stage than for the testes. During a growth spurt, the penis gets larger (both longer and wider) and the glans, or head of the penis, becomes more developed. A grown man's penis is usually between 3 and 4 inches (7.5–10 centimeters) long when flaccid.

Under certain conditions, for instance coming into contact with cold water or being out during cold weather, or if the man is afraid or tired, the penis can temporarily shrivel somewhat. Old age, however, can cause it to become permanently a bit smaller in size.

A WOMAN'S BODY

Muscles and fat Deposition of fat on the breasts, hips, thighs, and buttocks begins when a girl is about nine to ten. Later on, when she is about 15 to 17, more fat appears in the same areas. While her hips become rounded and swelling, the waist becomes curved and well defined. Some women develop stretch marks – faint purplish or white lines – on their skin at this time. This happens when the skin is stretched too much during this period of rapid growth.

The genitals A man's genitals lie on the surface of his body where they are easily seen and handled. A woman's genitals, however, are relatively inaccessible, more numerous, and fairly complex in design. Just as in other areas of human anatomy, the genitals of women are individual; they come in a variety of shapes, sizes, colors, and textures (see also p. 14).

Breasts The breasts are a symbol of feminine identity, forming part of the body image. Although their natural function is to nourish an infant, they are often far more highly regarded by society as a source of eroticism, a symbol of femininity, a determinant of fashion, and a measure of a woman's beauty.

The breasts, or mammary glands, are modified sweat glands. Each woman's breasts are unique in their size, shape, and appearance, and this variation not only occurs between women but in the same woman at different times of her life, that is during the menstrual cycle, pregnancy, and lactation. One breast is very often larger than the other.

In the center of the breast is a ring of skin called the areola; the nipple sits in its center. The nipple and areola can range in color from a light pink to a brownish black.

SEXUAL ANATOMY

There's no doubt that an awareness of and familiarity with sexual anatomy can make you a better lover. Knowing where your partner's most sensitive areas are, how they are likely to respond to stimulation and touch – and what happens when they do – enables you to give him or her maximum pleasure. And, if you realize that your partner is an individual who certainly will respond to particular caresses, perhaps in a very individual way, your lovemaking will become much more effective and mutually satisfying.

YOUR GENITALS ARE UNIQUE

Men find it somewhat easier to understand their own sexual anatomy since their sexual organs hang outside the body and are clearly and constantly visible. But both women and men are less familiar with female anatomy, and this is because so many of the important parts lie hidden within a woman's body.

Just as in other areas of anatomy, the genitals of men and women are individual; they come in a range of shapes and sizes. Normal variation means that a few women have exceptionally large or small vaginas, just as the occasional man has an exceptionally large or small penis. Women rarely express dissatisfaction with the size and shape of their external genitals – maybe because comparison with those of other women is not usual, so ignorance is bliss. However, the vast majority of men are dissatisfied with the quality of their sex organs, and many feel that a small or average penis is a drawback to their sexual value.

Fortunately, there are many women who couldn't care less or who hardly notice the size of their partner's penis. Indeed, some women are physically uncomfortable with a big penis; a smaller penis is easier for a woman to take when it comes to oral sex, for instance. Furthermore, many of a woman's sensations from intercourse come from the clitoris and from the nerve endings that are mainly in the first couple of inches of the vagina, so the length of the penis really is irrelevant. It is a man's skill and patience as a lover, not the size of his penis, that is responsible for giving his partner sexual satisfaction.

On the other hand, many women are dissatisfied with their breasts and it may be that some of the dissatisfaction that both sexes have regarding their visible anatomy is the result of foreshortened viewing; both penises and breasts are normally viewed by their owners from the top down. What really matters, though, is taking pride and delight in your own individuality – not worrying about what your genitals look like compared with other people's – and that everything functions normally.

A MAN'S SEX ORGANS

THE PENIS

No organ has more myths attached to it than the penis. It has been praised, blamed, and misrepresented in literature, art, and legend since time immemorial. These phallic fallacies have become firmly fixed in our culture, thereby influencing our attitudes and behavior.

The penis has two functions – urination and the depositing of semen in the vagina – but it is the role of the penis as the organ responsible for orgasm in both men and women that has achieved mythical status.

Although they vary in length, the average penis measures 3¾ inches (9.5 centimeters) in its flaccid state. It is composed of erectile tissue arranged in three cylindrical columns. The column that is underneath expands at the end of the penis to form the glans. Through the center of this column runs the urethra, a narrow tube carrying semen (and urine) out of the body through an opening at the tip of the glans. When a man has an erection, and for a few minutes after he has ejaculated, the urethra becomes compressed so that he can't urinate, although semen can get through.

The penis is covered by muscles and filled with a rich network of blood vessels and blood spaces; the latter remain empty when the penis is flaccid but have the potential to fill and expand with blood during erection.

The expanded glans is demarcated from the main shaft of the penis by an indentation that runs around its head, and the skin on the shaft of the penis forms a fold (the foreskin) that extends to cover the glans. On its lower side, the fold is tethered to the inner surface of the glans by the frenulum. For many men, this tiny band of skin is their most sensitive part and, if stimulated, may quickly arouse them.

At birth, the foreskin is attached to the glans; starting in infancy, it gradually separates. The foreskin may be removed by circumcision. There is no truth in the notion that an uncircumcised man can control ejaculation more effectively than a man who is circumcised. This myth is founded on the widespread misconception that the glans of the circumcised penis is more sensitive to touch than the glans covered most of the time by a foreskin. During intercourse, the foreskin retracts exposing the glans exactly as for a circumcised glans.

The skin of the penis is thin, stretchy, without fat, and loosely attached to the underlying tissues. The penis is richly supplied with sensory nerves and nerves from the autonomic nervous system.

CHANGES TO PENIS SIZE

When a man is sexually aroused, the penis normally increases in length – an extra 2¾–3¼ inches (7–8 centimeters) – and stiffness. Erection may take place in a few seconds, and is due to a very great increase in blood flow into the penis. The blood spaces fill with blood, which is prevented from draining away into the veins by swollen arteries that compress them; the erection is thus maintained until after ejaculation.

It is widely accepted that the larger the penis, the more effective a man will be as a sexual partner. This delusion (since it is delusion), that penile size is related to sexual potency, is based on yet another phallic fallacy: that when a larger penis becomes erect it achieves a bigger size than a smaller penis upon erection. But this is not the case. In the laboratory of researchers Masters and Johnson, men whose penises were 3–3½ inches (7.5–9 centimeters) long in the flaccid state increased by an average of 3–3¼ inches (7.5–8 centimeters) when fully erect, which essentially doubled the smaller organs in length over flaccid size standards. In contrast, in the men whose organs were significantly larger in the flaccid state – 4–4¾ inches (10–11.5 centimeters) – penile length increased by an average of only 2¾–3 inches (7–7.5 centimeters) when fully erect.

THE SCROTUM

The scrotum is the pouch of skin situated below the root of the penis that houses the testes. It's divided by a fibrous sheet and this division can be seen on the surface of the scrotum as a ridge. The skin of the scrotum is dark and thin and contains numerous sebaceous glands and sparse hairs. Under the skin is a smooth muscle that contracts in response to cold, or vigorous exercise; its contraction makes the scrotum smaller and its skin wrinkled.

THE TESTES

The testes are smooth, oval structures that are compressed from side to side like broad beans. The left testis may be slightly lower than the right. Each testis is inside a sac and has four coverings that correspond to the various layers of the abdominal wall; these are carried down into the scrotal sac when the testis migrates from inside the abdomen just before birth. Small muscles control the height of the testes. Their position may change according to the level of a man's sexual arousal, his emotions, and the temperature of the scrotum, among

other things. Sperm develop normally only if they are produced at a temperature two or three degrees lower than the rest of the body. The testes provide the necessary temperature because they are "outside" the body.

The two functions of the testis are to produce sperm and male hormones or androgens, primarily testosterone. A fine tube carries sperm developed in the testis to the epididymis, where it is stored. This comma-shaped structure is stuck to the rear surface of the testis and is, in effect, an extensively coiled duct.

The vas deferens carries sperm via the spermatic cord into the pelvis, where it joins the back of the bladder with the seminal vesicle. Each duct (see above) then continues downward and, joined by the duct of the seminal vesicle, forms the ejaculatory duct, which runs on through the body of the prostate and enters the urethra inside the prostate gland. Each seminal vesicle contains a small quantity of sticky fluid in which the sperm are supported and nourished, and which forms the ejaculate.

THE PROSTATE

The prostate is a fibrous, muscular, and glandular organ shaped like a chestnut. It produces secretions that form part of the seminal fluid during ejaculation. It is contained in a fibrous capsule and sits just below the neck of the bladder. The male urethra passes right through the center of the prostate. If the prostate gland enlarges, the urethral outlet may be narrowed. This leads to difficulty in urinating, dribbling, and poor stream (a not uncommon condition in men over 55 years of age). Beyond the prostate are the Cowper's glands, which add lubricant to the seminal fluid prior to ejaculation.

A WOMAN'S SEX ORGANS

THE VULVA

A woman's external and visible genitalia are known as the vulva or pudendum. It is a very erotic, sensitive area, which also serves to protect the vaginal and urethral openings. The fatty tissue and skin at the front of the vulva is the mons pubis, or mound of Venus; it covers where the pelvic bones join at the front, and acts as a cushion during intercourse. In the mature female, it is covered by hair.

The most superficial structures of the vulva, the labia majora, extend forward from the anus and fuse at the front in the mons pubis. These "lips" are two-fold, and usually lie together and conceal the other external genital organs. They are composed of fibrous and fatty tissue, and carry hair follicles as well as sebaceous and apocrine (sweat) glands. The latter give rise to a special form of odorous sweat, which is a sexual chemical attractant.

The labia minora are folds of skin that lie between the labia majora. They have many sebaceous glands that produce sebum, which lubricates the skin and, combined with the secretions from the vagina and sweat glands, forms a waterproof protective covering against urine, bacteria, and menstrual blood.

The size and shape of these lips vary greatly and, like the labia majora, one is usually larger than the other. They may be hidden by the labia majora or project forward. During sexual excitement they become engorged, change color, and increase in thickness.

THE CLITORIS

The clitoris (the most sensitive organ of the vulva) is the female equivalent of the penis, with the same component parts but in miniature. In anatomical and physiological terms, the clitoris is a unique organ. There is no organ in the human male that acts solely as a receptor and transmitter of sensual stimuli, purely to initiate or elevate levels of sexual tension and excitement.

The body of the clitoris is ¾ to 1¼ inches (2 to 3 centimeters) long and is acutely bent back on itself. The top of the clitoris is covered by a sensitive membrane that contains many receptive nerve endings. During intercourse, the clitoris doubles in size and becomes erect – in exactly the same way as the penis. The length of the whole clitoris, including the shaft and glans, varies greatly depending on stimulation by hormones during puberty.

THE HYMEN

During childhood, the hymen – a thin membrane – guards the opening to the vagina. It is normally perforated and allows the escape of menstrual blood. Its thickness and stiffness vary from woman to woman; in rare cases it is so strong and resistant that intercourse is difficult; the hymen must then be cut under local anesthetic. Usually, however, it is torn during various childhood activities such as bicycling or horseback riding, or by the use of tampons. Even if intact, it is rarely as painful during first penetration as literature would have us believe.

THE VAGINA

The vagina is a potential, rather than an actual space. It is a fibromuscular tube about 3¼ inches (8 centimeters) long, but its size is variable, and so capable of distortion that any normal vagina can accommodate any size of penis with ease. If penetration happens before expansion of the vagina in length and diameter has fully developed, a woman may experience initial difficulty in accommodating the erect penis. But vaginal expansion continues rapidly so that the penis – regardless of its size – is accommodated within a few thrusts.

As excitement increases, the vagina normally overextends in circumference as well as length. This elliptical vaginal expansion accounts for some loss of stimulation for the penis, and reduces vaginal sensation for the woman.

INSIDE THE VAGINA

The projection of the cervix allows the space of the vaginal vault to be divided into front, back, and lateral fornices. The cervix enters the vault through the upper part of the front vaginal wall and as a result, the front wall is shorter than the rear wall and the rear fornix is much deeper than the one in front. This arrangement favors the passage of sperm into the cervix during intercourse because, when a woman lies on her back, the opening of the cervix is not only directly exposed to semen but is bathed by the pool of ejaculate that forms in the rear fornix in which it rests. During intercourse, it is this rear fornix that takes the brunt of penile thrusting and so protects the cervix from injury.

The lining of the vagina is thick and thrown into prominent folds. The lining cells of the vagina contain glycogen, a kind of starch. The fermentation action of bacteria, which normally live in the vagina, on the glycogen produces lactic acid that renders the fluid in the vagina on the acid side of normal. This acid environment is necessary to maintain the health of the vagina and to deter bacterial growth. Any interference with this delicate ecological balance, for instance, vaginal douches, can cause irritation, inflammation, discharge, and allergic reactions.

The lining of the vagina does not contain glands, even though the vagina lubricates itself with a kind of sweat when a woman becomes sexually aroused. Under normal circumstances, cells that are routinely shed from the lining of the vagina, mucus secreted from the cervix, and vaginal sweating all combine to form the normal colorless and odorless vaginal discharge.

Inside the top of the vagina, lying directly behind the pubic bone, is said to be an area of erectile tissue that, when stimulated, produces a different type of orgasm. This area, called the "G" spot, is discussed in more detail on page 24.

THE GREATER VESTIBULAR GLANDS AND URETHRA

The greater vestibular glands, also called Bartholin's glands, lie behind and slightly to the side of the vagina. The ducts of these glands open into the angle between the labia minora and the ring of the hymen and carry lubricating mucus to the vaginal opening and the vulva's inner parts.

The urethra is embedded within the substance of the lower half of the front vaginal wall. Bruising of this wall can therefore result in inflammation of the urethra and an ascending infection of the bladder (cystitis). The middle third of the rear wall of the vagina is closely related to the rectum, and the muscles that form the pelvic floor, called the levators, blend with the middle part of the sides of the vagina to form the most crucial support of the vaginal structure.

SEXUAL RESPONSE

If you are attuned to your body, you know that your sexual responses have identifiable stages – desire, arousal, climax, and resolution – and that these stages are accompanied by bodily changes. What is less well known is that although these stages occur in men and women in the same order, and in much the same way, there are vital differences. For women the

A WOMAN'S RESPONSE TO SEX

Exciting a woman brings about visible changes in many different parts of the body. As she becomes sexually aroused, a woman's breathing becomes more rapid, and her heart beats more quickly. Her lips become pink, the pupils of her eyes dilate, and her nipples become erect and stiffen. As excitement climbs, her skin becomes pink and flushed, it begins to sweat, and her breasts swell as they become engorged with blood.

THE VAGINA BECOMES MOIST

A woman's first response to sexual stimulation, which invariably must be touch, is vaginal lubrication, which can appear within 10–30 seconds of her becoming excited. Individual droplets of mucuslike material appear at intervals throughout the folds of the vaginal walls – a form of sweating. While the clitoris is the main focus of a woman's sexual response, its reaction is slower, and nowhere near as fast as a penile erection.

As sexual excitement increases, the droplets fuse together to form a smooth, lubricating coat over the entire barrel of the vagina, making penetration by a penis extremely easy. This lubricating mucus can appear in the most copious amounts, and it is thought to originate from an enormously increased blood supply, which is almost simultaneous with the onset of sexual excitement. No

other source has been discovered. The response is almost certainly not a hormonal one, since it occurs in women who have had a complete hysterectomy.

THE CLITORIS RESPONDS

The speed of response by the clitoris depends on whether it is stimulated directly or indirectly. The most rapid response depends on direct stimulation of the clitoral body or the mons area. Indirect stimulation, which includes manipulation of other erogenous zones such as the breasts or vagina without direct clitoral contact, has a definite but certainly slower response.

The only form of direct stimulation is touch – by the fingers, mouth, or erect penis – and most women require touch in addition to penetration to achieve an orgasm. Because of its position, the clitoris is not stimulated directly during intercourse, so movements of the penis on its own are often insufficient to excite the clitoris to orgasm. However, indirect stimulation of the clitoris does develop with penile thrusting, the body being pulled downward and then the hood being released.

THE VAGINA CHANGES

As sexual excitement increases, the shape of the vagina changes in readiness for penetration. The inner two-thirds of changes are usually initiated by different stimuli and take a longer time to occur, but they last longer, and can be repeated more quickly. The changes are reversible if either party is distracted.

Desire begins in the brain, which then sends messages to the body that result in a variety of changes indicating arousal. Arousal, if prolonged sufficiently, leads to climax, and with orgasm, muscular tension is released and the flow of blood to the pelvis is reversed.

the vaginal barrel lengthens and distends; in highly excited women, this distension is quite marked. The cervix and uterus are pulled backward and upward into the pelvis, further expanding the upper end of the vagina.

At the same time, the color of the vaginal walls changes. The vagina is normally a deep pink, but this color slowly alters to a darker purplish hue as the blood supply to the vagina increases.

In the preorgasmic state, the vagina is so distended that all the folds of the wall are stretched and flattened, and the lining becomes thin. In the plateau phase, the outer third of the vagina swells with blood, and this distension may be so great that the lower part of the vagina is reduced by at least one-third. In addition, an increase in blood supply results in enlarged labia minora and majora, which become separated, elevated, and turned out.

ORGASM OCCURS

It has never been possible to study the orgasmic changes in the clitoris due to its retraction beneath the hood formed by the labia minora. The changes in the vagina, however, are much easier to study. The outer one-third contracts regularly during orgasm, with normally three to five, up to a maximum of 10 to 15, contractions at 0.8-second intervals. After the initial three to six contractions,

the space between them lengthens. Each contraction is intensely pleasurable; these fantastic sensations fall away as the contractions lessen.

How long orgasmic contractions last, their degree, and the interval between them vary among women and from one orgasm to another. Occasionally, with the highest tension levels, orgasm may start with a single deep contraction that lasts two to four seconds before muscle spasm develops into the regular contraction lasting less than a second.

During orgasm, the uterine muscle contracts, and the fornices expand, forming a tent to receive the sperm.

A RETURN TO NORMAL

After orgasm it can take a considerable time for the vagina to return to its normal appearance. As long as 10 to 15 minutes may elapse before the basic coloration returns to the vagina and the folds reappear.

The clitoris returns to its normal overhanging position within five to ten seconds after orgasmic contractions have ceased, and the discoloration of the labia minora disappears just as quickly. Detumescence of the clitoral glans is a relatively slow process and may last five to ten minutes; in some women, it may take as long as 30 minutes. If orgasm isn't reached, swelling of the clitoris may last for several hours after sexual activity.

A MAN'S RESPONSE TO SEX

When a man becomes excited, his reactions, just like a woman's, are not confined solely to his sex organs. Excitement begins in the brain, when a man becomes aroused by something either real or imagined. A man is aroused by mainly visual stimuli; clothing and makeup as well as the sight of naked or semi-naked female bodies turn him on. A man readily becomes conditioned by his experiences; objects or circumstances associated with sex may elicit arousal, also. In this way, without any physical contact, male arousal occurs frequently and rapidly.

THE PENIS BECOMES ERECT

Messages from the brain travel down the spinal cord to the genitals and shut off the outflow of blood from the penis, and this brings about an erection. A man's usually limp, downward-hanging organ becomes a rigid, upward-pointing, dusky-colored, throbbing one with prominent veins.

By carefully controlling the variation and intensity of stimulative techniques, erection can be maintained for extended periods; it can be partially lost and rapidly regained many times during a long period of stimulation.

Erection can be easily interrupted by nonsexual stimuli, even though sexual stimulation is continued. Any form of mental distraction, a sudden loud noise, or a change in temperature or lighting, may result in partial, or even complete, loss of erection.

BODILY CHANGES OCCUR

In addition to making the penis become erect, the increased blood supply leads also to reddening and mottling of the skin in about a quarter of all men. This "sex flush" starts in the lower abdomen and spreads over the skin of the chest, neck, and face. It may appear on the shoulders, forearms, and thighs and, when fully developed, may even look like measles. Its appearance is always evidence of high levels of sexual excitement. After ejaculation, the sex flush disappears very rapidly.

A man's breast, like a woman's breast, is very responsive to sexual stimulation. Although the pattern is inconsistent, nipple swelling and erection, which may develop without direct contact and can last for an hour after ejaculation, occurs frequently. Many women are not aware that a man's nipples, and even his chest, can become erogenous zones if they are given enough stimulation.

A man's heart rate increases with sexual excitement, and his respiratory rate and blood pressure also rise. His scrotum thickens and his testes will be drawn closer to his body. Many men sweat involuntarily immediately after ejaculation, but this is not proportional to the amount of physical exertion during intercourse. Sweating is usually confined to the soles of the feet and the palms of the hands but may appear on the trunk, head, face, and neck.

PRIOR TO ORGASM

Right before orgasm there is a sense of ejaculatory inevitability for an instant. Many men have described the onset of this sensation as "feeling the ejaculation coming." From the onset of this sensation, there is a brief interval, two to three seconds at the most, during which a man feels the ejaculation coming but is no longer able to prevent, delay, or in any way control the process. This experience of inevitability develops as seminal fluid is collecting in the prostatic urethra, just before the actual emission of seminal fluid begins. While a woman's orgasm can be interrupted by extraneous stimuli, once initiated, a man's orgasm cannot be delayed until emission has been completed.

Just prior to ejaculation, the glans may change color; its mottled, reddish purple color may become darker. (This is reminiscent of the preorgasmic discoloration of the labia minora in a woman.) A drop of fluid may form at the urethral opening of the penis prior to ejaculation. This is not seminal fluid but secretions from Cowper's glands (see p. 13). The size of the testes increases slightly and they also become elevated. At this point, it is increasingly difficult for the penis to return to its resting state without ejaculation.

Muscle contractions occur at a late stage of sexual excitement and may be involuntary or voluntary, depending on body position. Spasms of a man's hands and feet can occur – rarely if the man is on top – but more commonly when he is supine.

ORGASM OCCURS

Regularly recurring contractions of both the urethra and the deep muscles of the penis result inevitably in ejaculation and the exquisitely pleasant sensations of orgasm. The entire length of the penile urethra contracts rhythmically, forcing seminal fluid from the full length of the penis under pressure, often from some distance away. When ejaculation occurs, contractions of the rectal sphincter are experienced at the same time as the expulsive contractions of the urethra.

The penis contracts similarly to the vagina during orgasm: the contractions start at intervals of 0.8 seconds and, after three or four major expulsions, they are rapidly reduced in frequency and expulsive force. Minor contractions of the penile urethra may continue for several seconds in an irregular manner, projecting a minimal amount of seminal fluid under little, if any, force.

If a man has not had intercourse for several days he usually ejaculates a larger volume of seminal fluid than when he is more sexually active. A larger volume can be more pleasurable than a lower volume, and this may account for a man's greater pleasure after a significant period of continence than after repeated orgasms. This pattern is the opposite to that reported by women who, as a rule, enjoy the second or third orgasm most.

Orgasm and ejaculation are two separate processes and may or may not occur at the same time. One can occur without the other. Orgasm involves the sudden pleasurable sensations and release of tension that usually occur in the genital area and elsewhere in the body; ejaculation involves the discharge of seminal fluid from the penis. A man may ejaculate as the result of sexual stimulation but not experience the sensation of orgasm. Less frequently, a man may have an orgasm but not ejaculate. Most men who experience multiple orgasms ejaculate only once.

Normally, the penis becomes flaccid following intercourse and a man will not get another erection for some time, particularly if a man removes his penis from his partner's vagina immediately following ejaculation. Once the penis returns to its normal size, the man will relax and very often feel sleepy.

ORGASM

Orgasm, the climax of sensation, is a uniquely human experience. For men, orgasm depends almost entirely on the stimulation of the penis, either by hand or mouth, as well as the vaginal walls, and is usually, although not always, accompanied by ejaculation of seminal fluid. For women, clitoral stimulation and movement of the penis within the vagina, prolonged through skill and experience, produce these intense feelings. Women can reach orgasm in other ways too – for instance, by manual or oral stimulation of the clitoris, vagina, or "G" spot. About one woman in ten experiences the emission of fluid from the urethra with orgasm. It is thought that this fluid comes from the Skene's glands, which run alongside the urethra, since it is not urine or vaginal mucus.

Orgasms vary: mood, level of energy or fatigue, amount and type of loveplay, the level of mutual trust, and what is happening in either partner's life, all have their effect on the sensation. And not every sexual experience can, nor should, end in orgasm; there are times when orgasms are a natural outcome of sexual activities and other times when lovers will have orgasms only if they really work at them.

A MAN'S ORGASM

Physical response As the engorged reproductive glands spurt out their contents into the part of the urethra that runs through the prostate, expanding it as they do so, exquisitely pleasant sensations are produced. A series of four or five contractions, at the rate of one every 0.8 seconds, follows as the man ejaculates the semen in store.

Some men tend to have extremely powerful physical reactions during their orgasms: they may moan and groan, contort their faces and bodies, and sometimes even scare their partners by their cataclysmic reactions. On the other hand, there are men who have very tranquil, quiet orgasms, leaving their partners wondering whether they have come at all. Most men probably experience a range of intensities between these two extreme reactions.

A WOMAN'S ORGASM

Physical response How long orgasmic contractions last, their level of intensity, and the space between them vary from woman to woman and from one orgasm to another. Some women experience a high peak of pleasure that fades away rapidly, while others feel orgasm as a more widespread, warm, internal sensation; some arrive at a peak, which subsides gradually into a series of pleasurable plateaus.

In response to orgasm, a woman may arch her body and tense her muscles, and her face may be pulled into a grimace. She may scream, cry out, or bite her lips. Alternatively, she may be silent, and you may simply observe a quickening of excitement, and feel some involuntary hip movements, muscle contractions in the genital area, and a general release of tension as the orgasm subsides.

— A MAN'S ORGASM —

Types We're just beginning to discover that like women, men have a variety of orgasms with the added differences that different patterns of ejaculation can provide. There is no right way for a man to ejaculate or to have an orgasm.

The main source of pleasure is often a powerful ejaculation. On the other hand, the sensations of orgasm may be felt for a long time with the ejaculation experience almost an anticlimax. On other occasions, a man may experience several continued orgasmic sensations long after he has ejaculated, or he may experience a pattern similar to the multiple orgasms of women – a series of fairly closely spaced mini-orgasms with ejaculation occurring at the last one.

Multiple orgasm After a major orgasm, most men experience a refractory period during which further sexual stimulation will not lead to an erection. Many males under the age of 30, however, have the ability to ejaculate frequently with only short resting periods. While men are resistant to sexual stimuli immediately after ejaculation, with practice and learned control, many men can extend their sexual cycles and enjoy several mini-orgasms before a final climax.

After experiencing orgasm a man's emotional reactions generally tend to reflect the relationship that he has with his partner. Feelings of satisfaction, contentment, and happiness usually result from a loving relationship, while sadness, depression, and a drained feeling frequently follow where intimacy and understanding are missing, as in one-night stands. The majority of men, too, often feel mentally exhausted after orgasm, with the common result that sleep readily ensues.

— A WOMAN'S ORGASM —

Types Masters and Johnson declared categorically that the female orgasm originates in the clitoris and that there is not a second kind of orgasm that originates in the vagina. Research into the personal experience of many women does, however, suggest, at the very least, that there is a type of orgasm that starts in the clitoris and spreads down into the vagina. This results in a more powerful climax than when the orgasm involves the clitoris alone. This kind of orgasm is said to result from stimulation of the "G" spot (see p. 24) and is reputed to be a deep, powerful, prolonged sensation that is accompanied by contractions of the vagina, uterus, and pelvic organs. Women state that it is truly transporting and brings them in closer union with their partners than any other orgasm.

Multiple orgasm A major difference between the sexes is that many more women are capable of experiencing more than one orgasm during a single sexual act. By holding back from the brink or preventing themselves from ever reaching orgasm, men should be able to prolong coitus and give more than one orgasm to their partners. Instead of moving to the resolution stage, those women able to have multiple orgasms remain at the plateau phase in a highly aroused state, and from there they can be stimulated to orgasm quickly and repeatedly.

After orgasm, women are less prone to the slightly depressed feelings that men often experience, and the majority welcome further loving attentions from their partners. A very few women experience a drifting into a mild form of unconsciousness, poetically known as the "little death," after orgasm.

MAN'S SEXUAL RESPONSE

After only a few minutes of stimulation, excitement increases quickly until the man reaches the plateau phase, where he can remain for any length of time according to his desires. Most men have to remain here for several minutes, sometimes 30, but on average about 15, until their partners catch up and penetration becomes mutually desirable. Once inside, a man's sexual pleasure increases markedly, especially as thrusting movements bring him step by step to the point of no return and an intensely pleasurable moment with orgasm and ejaculation. After this, excitement drops steeply, the penis becomes flaccid, and the man enters the refractory period, a variable time during which an erection is no longer possible.

MAN'S EXPERIENCE

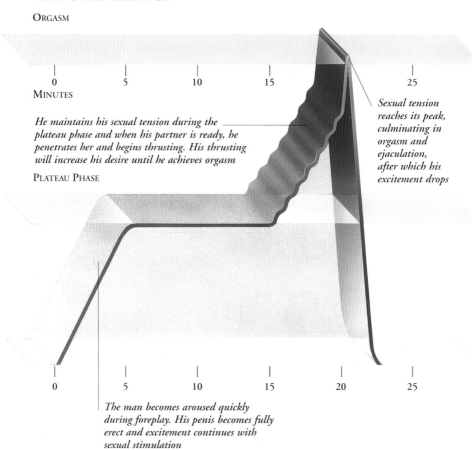

ORGASM

| | | | | | |
| 0 | 5 | 10 | 15 | | 25 |

MINUTES

Sexual tension reaches its peak, culminating in orgasm and ejaculation, after which his excitement drops

He maintains his sexual tension during the plateau phase and when his partner is ready, he penetrates her and begins thrusting. His thrusting will increase his desire until he achieves orgasm

PLATEAU PHASE

| | | | | | |
| 0 | 5 | 10 | 15 | 20 | 25 |

The man becomes aroused quickly during foreplay. His penis becomes fully erect and excitement continues with sexual stimulation

WOMAN'S SEXUAL RESPONSE

Sexual tension in the initial stage increases more slowly in women than men, frequently taking 20 or 25 minutes but, on average, 15 minutes. The more varied and stimulating the foreplay, the more rapidly a woman passes through this initial arousal phase. Her pleasure then rises in a parallel and incremental fashion with the thrusting of the penis within her vagina. If direct stimulation of the clitoris is maintained simultaneously throughout this period, a woman can proceed quickly to the point of orgasm. After orgasm there is a slow and gradual return to normality, often extending up to half an hour. During this resolution phase, the breasts return to their normal size and the swelling of the labia diminishes.

WOMAN'S EXPERIENCE

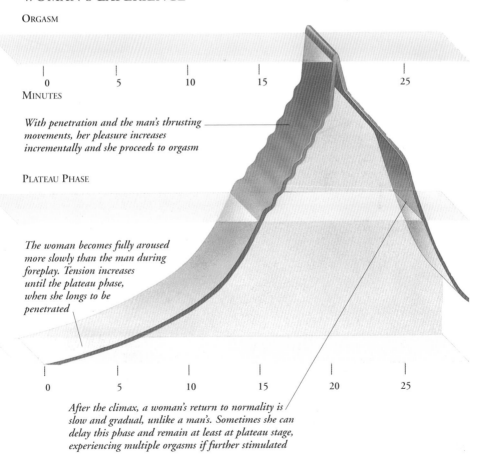

ORGASM

| | | | | | |
|0|5|10|15| |25|

MINUTES

With penetration and the man's thrusting movements, her pleasure increases incrementally and she proceeds to orgasm

PLATEAU PHASE

The woman becomes fully aroused more slowly than the man during foreplay. Tension increases until the plateau phase, when she longs to be penetrated

| | | | | | |
|0|5|10|15|20|25|

After the climax, a woman's return to normality is slow and gradual, unlike a man's. Sometimes she can delay this phase and remain at least at plateau stage, experiencing multiple orgasms if further stimulated

THE "G" SPOT

In Germany in the 1940s an obstetrician and gynecologist called Ernst Grafenburg, researching new methods of birth control, claimed to have discovered a new, internal zone of erogenous feeling in the women he was studying. This sparked a controversy, which has become more prevalent in recent years, concerning whether or not these male and female "G" (Grafenburg) spots in fact exist.

There seems to be little doubt that there is a hidden area, at least in some men and women, which when stimulated, produces intense excitement and orgasm; in women this has become known as the "G" spot, and in men has been identified as the prostate gland. While it is

Stimulating the "G" spot
A face-to-face, sitting position, such as the one shown here, enables the penis to stimulate the front wall of the vagina, where the female "G" spot is located.

physiologically undeniable that men have a prostate gland, pathologists have failed to find the "G" spot (which feels like a small bean when stimulated) when performing autopsies on females. Several experts believe that it is possible that the "G" spot exists only in some women; others believe simply that the front wall of the vagina is extremely sensitive and when stimulated can produce an orgasm in some women; others dismiss the whole notion as complete nonsense and claim that the entire controversy causes unnecessary feelings of inadequacy and anxiety among both men and women.

Self-discovery is really the only way you can find out if the "G" spot can produce intense pleasure for you or whether, as for some people, it is a complete waste of time.

THE MALE "G" SPOT

The male "G" spot has been identified as the prostate gland. It is situated (like the female "G" spot) around the urethra at the neck of the bladder. The prostate gland has a physiological function: helping produce the fluid that carries sperm into the vagina during sexual intercourse. Many men discover that stimulation of the prostate before or during intercourse can result in an extremely intense orgasm, during which they ejaculate in a gentle stream rather than in spurts.

It is very difficult for a man to find his own "G" spot, or prostate gland. The best position for discovering the gland yourself is to lie on your back with your knees bent and your feet flat on the floor, or with your knees drawn up to your chest. Insert your thumb into the anus and press against the front wall. Your prostate should feel like a firm mass about the size of a walnut, and when it is stimulated, it should produce feelings of intense sexual excitement.

THE FEMALE "G" SPOT

The "G" spot appears to be a small cluster of nerve endings, glands, ducts, and blood vessels sited around a woman's urethra, or urinary tract. This area cannot normally be felt when the woman is unaroused, only becoming distinguishable as a specific area during deep vaginal stimulation. When this happens it swells, sometimes very rapidly, and a small mass with distinct edges stands out from the vaginal wall. Since it seems to have no function other than helping a woman achieve a high degree of sexual fulfillment and, at orgasm, can appear to "ejaculate" a clear liquid similar in composition to that created by the prostate, some experts think that the "G" spot is a rudimentary form of the male prostate gland.

The easiest way to find your "G" spot is to sit or squat, because lying down positions the relevant spot farther away. The first time you stimulate your "G" spot can feel like wanting to urinate, so it is a good idea to start your explorations while sitting on the toilet. Once your bladder is empty, you will know that the sensation is caused by the "G" spot, and not by having a full bladder.

THE MALE "G" SPOT

The anus is delicate, unused to having things inserted into it, and is not a naturally lubricating organ. Therefore, make sure that fingernails are short and that fingers are well lubricated so as not to cause damage.

If you want your partner to stimulate you, lie down on your back and have her gently insert a finger into your anus. Allow yourself enough time to become accustomed to having her finger there, then have her feel up the front rectal wall until she finds your prostate and massages it firmly. Then she can stroke the gland in a downward direction. This can be tiring to both partners but is made a little easier for you if you pull your knees back towards your chest. Without her even touching your penis you will probably become erect and have an orgasm.

This maneuver is not as "messy" as a woman may perhaps think, since unless you are constipated, there are no feces in your lower rectum. Your partner must, however, wash her fingers at once and must not touch inside her vagina, or bacteria could be transferred to her from your anus. Some women feel better if they use a disposable plastic glove, especially since it gives some protection against transmitting the AIDS virus.

Some women like to fellate their partners at the same time as massaging the prostate, and you might suggest this to your partner as well.

THE FEMALE "G" SPOT

Using your fingers, apply firm upward pressure on the front of the internal vaginal wall, perhaps pressing down simultaneously with the other hand on the outside of the abdomen. As it becomes stimulated, the spot should start to swell and will feel like a lump between the fingers inside and outside your vagina. Extremely pleasurable contractions may sweep through the uterus and you may experience a deep, satisfying orgasm, which will feel totally different from a clitoral orgasm.

At this point you may also find that you ejaculate a small amount of clear fluid from the urethra. This is not urine, despite its appearance.

Since your partner can reach the spot more easily, it may be more effective if he stimulates you. Lie down on a bed with two firm pillows underneath your hips, with your legs slightly apart, and your bottom a little in the air. Your partner can lie down, lean close against you, gently insert two fingers (palm down), and stroke the front vaginal wall.

Sexual positions that produce "G" spot stimulation are the woman-on-top and the rear-entry positions. When a woman is on top of a man, she can control the depth and direction of her partner's penis and can move forward or from side-to-side to guide it to the place that feels best for her. In rear-entry positions, the penis is rubbing directly on the front wall of the vagina in which the "G" spot is located.

A man can help his partner by moving his own body and pressing the base of his penis to make sure that its head makes full contact with the "G" spot. These movements can result in a series of intense orgasms for both partners.

ATTRACTION AND DESIRE

Many myths exist as to what men and women find
attractive in each other – there is no proof, for example,
that gentleman prefer blondes – but scientists believe that
many of the associations we form in infancy help
determine whom we choose as sexual partners, or soul
mates, and that patterns laying down tendencies for love
relationships are etched deeply into our brains.
The infinite range of human experience through holding,
touching, feeling, stimulating, trusting, talking, and
listening is involved in the sexual attraction of
a loving couple and their desire for each other.

ATTRACTING A PARTNER

Both our ability to love and our style of loving begin to develop from the moment we're born. Scientists believe that many of the associations we form in infancy help determine whom we choose as sexual partners, or soul mates, and that patterns that lay down tendencies for love relations are etched into our brains.

I can show you how this might be so by looking at how just one of the five senses – smell – predetermines a particular choice. Each of us, even in our highly deodorized society, has a unique odor that is the sum of our glandular secretions – a "smell signature." Whether our smell signature is attractive to other people – for instance, because it reminds them happily of their mothers – or is off-putting because it reminds them of detested ex-spouses, say, depends on those people's own associations. Associations are linked to smell because the olfactory bulb involved with smell reception feeds into the part of the brain that is intimately linked with emotion and affective memory.

In the same way, we can learn to like the smells of our loved ones. Studies have shown that lovers can pick each other out of a group solely by their unique aromatic signatures (and that is how babies first bond with their mothers). If we lose our ability to smell, we normally suffer a pronounced slump in sex drive.

THE CHOICE OF A PARTNER

Highly personal patterns, like our individual smell associations, make it extremely difficult to generalize about attraction. Men and women, in general, are attracted to the sexual characteristics that separate them – for example, women's larger breasts, men's broader shoulders. Cultural expectations, too, have a large role to play; a man to whom a Caucasian woman would be attracted is probably very different from a Chinese woman's ideal partner. Age, social class, personality, and the qualities we are looking for in a particular partner also very much determine whether or not we find a person attractive.

Many myths exist as to what men and women find attractive in each other. There is no proof, for example, that gentlemen prefer blondes – studies have shown that dark-haired men prefer brunettes, and fair-haired men like brunettes and blondes equally. And, while men think women like men with hairy chests and large penises, most women mention attributes such as tenderness, affection, respect, sensuality, and kindness as a man's most attractive qualities. If pressed, women will admit generally to preferring dark-haired men of average build, with small buttocks, and a tall, slim physique; penis size is rarely mentioned.

WHAT WOMEN LOOK FOR IN MEN

The choice of a sexual partner is still determined very much by evolutionary patterns where women first looked for mates who could be relied upon. For that reason, physical appearance appears to be less important to women than personal qualities.

Age is also not such an important factor in a woman's choice of a man. Unlike men, who have a tendency to look for younger women, women can be attracted to men of all age groups.

Personality Confidence, assertiveness, independence, and dominance tend to be found appealing, as are reliability and faithfulness, and qualities that suggest warmth, intimacy, and attentiveness. Men who try to get on with women and talk freely and openly about what interests them, and use a soothing voice, are more successful with women.

Prowess Men who are successful at work or sports, and have the visible proof, are more likely than less able men to attract women.

Physical qualities A man who is fit and healthy, with a well-muscled, fairly lean body that is not weedy, and who may have some surprising feminine characteristic such as long eyelashes, is considered more attractive than a stereotyped muscle man. Women prefer men taller than themselves.

Personal characteristics Attractive features to women are a body cleansed of the sweat of the day and free of body odor; a genital area whose scent is not too pungent; well-cared-for hands; clean feet, and a fresh pair of socks daily; newly washed hair; a face that is either clean-shaven or with a shapely beard, and without a rash.

WHAT MEN LOOK FOR IN WOMEN

Men generally place a higher premium on physical appearance than women do. In surveys, physical attractiveness is at the top of the list. Women's bodies are often on display in advertising and magazines, and men have been conditioned to find certain attributes especially stimulating. Legs, for example, tend to be powerful attractants because they indicate the state of a woman's maturity; high-heeled shoes, stockings, and skin-tight pants emphasize their allure and reinforce their sexual imagery. A woman's more pronounced buttocks, narrow waist, bare shoulders, and lips all act as sexual signals, but her breasts are her most obvious turn-on. Men, however, differ in what they find attractive. Some men even describe themselves as leg, buttock, or breast men. By and large, men are attracted to women younger than themselves – perhaps a subconscious recognition of their child-bearing capacity.

Personality Desirable qualities cited by men are sympathy, gentleness, warmth, kindness, and cheerfulness. Erotic ability rates higher than domesticity.

Physical qualities A lean but still curvaceous outline is desired rather than thinness, or a more maternal figure. A narrow waist and long legs are admired by the majority of men; breast size and shape are individual tastes.

Personal characteristics Attractive qualities to men are a genital area that is not too pungent or whose natural smell is not masked by strong deodorants or other synthetic smells; shapely polished fingernails and well-cared-for hands; not too much body hair; clean, soft hair; clean-smelling breath.

MAKING ADVANCES

Sending out sexual messages requires directness as well as a certain degree of vulnerability. It nearly always requires self-esteem to take the knocks and rejections that we might possibly receive when we make an advance. We need to have a mixture of arrogance and humility to assume that someone would want to know us better, while remembering that many people might rather have nothing to do with us. We ask ourselves the questions: "Do I remember taking this risk before and was it comfortable or uncomfortable?" and "Am I prepared to take this risk again?" An encouraging thought is that it is rare for someone that you are very interested in to be entirely indifferent to you.

WHERE AND HOW TO MEET

Many people think that there are only certain social situations where sex can be on the agenda. However, this is not true; any situation can lend itself to sexual advances. Of course, in some situations, advances need to be subtle and very low-key; in fact, they need to be rather difficult to pick up unless the other person is sexually aware and alert.

Only someone with a closed mind would limit his or her horizons to parties, dinners, and social occasions. Sexual interest can be revealed at any time. For instance, a working business meeting between two sexually interested people, when each may be thrilled by the other's professional performance, can be an exciting and intriguing prelude to more open sexual overtures. Here, the enjoyment of a common job can greatly enhance sexual interest. Indeed, sexual interest grows more often in the day-to-day working environment than almost anywhere else.

While women rate discos and parties as the most likely way of meeting men with whom they would like a sexual relationship, reality is, in fact, quite different. Most people meet potential sexual partners through friends, and like any other form of friendship, most happy sexual relationships are based on friendship and on working or studying together. You can get to know someone better at work than in a disco. Furthermore, when looking very glamorous and affected by drink, we don't necessarily give a realistic picture of ourselves, nor are we able to get a true insight into a partner.

A less obvious advance could occur when you have lunch with or talk to someone over a period of time in a quiet spot. Glances are often exchanged and conversations may include messages with a double meaning, testing how interested the other person is. These interactions may just be in the form of play, but all of us do engage in them and establish brief "mini" bonds with many people.

SENDING OUT MESSAGES

The truth is we cannot help but communicate. Even if we are not actually speaking, we are giving out signals through the body. People are perceived as being friendly or unfriendly without a word being spoken. Body gestures give messages about subconscious emotions and are, therefore, a very direct form of communication. You can use them to see what others are thinking. They often belie what we are saying; probably, nonverbal gestures are more accurate in many situations than words themselves. And, as we gain awareness of nonverbal behavior and an interest in interpreting the body language of others, we become aware of our own bodily gestures, resulting in more effective outward communication.

EYE CONTACT

By far the most common initial sexual advance is eye contact. Our eyes meet with interest, with approbation; a very brief fantasy may occur – "I'm sure I would like to have a relationship with you. I will never talk to you but I think we could do something together" – and we may think about this anonymous message later. These encounters may take place in the street, walking down the hall at work, on the stairs, in an elevator, or at a traffic light, and they happen often. We do this every day of our lives, even if we are very happy with a partner. We seem to keep practicing attraction by sending at least mini-messages to test our abilities.

Eye contact is one of the simplest and most direct ways of showing someone that you are sexually interested in him or her, and by making eye contact, you make it easier for that person to respond to you.

Always look at the person you are talking to, not over his or her shoulder or down at the floor. To show interest in another, hold your glance longer than you would do in an ordinary social situation, but don't overdo it. Most people find intermittent eye contact – about five seconds out of every 30 – most comfortable and will probably drop their gaze if you look at them directly for too long. A person expresses interest if he or she returns your gaze steadily.

VERBAL COMMUNICATION

Conversation, too, whether at a casual encounter, an intimate dinner, or during the course of work, can be a huge sexual turn-on. Glances are often exchanged and conversations may include messages with a double meaning that test the interest of the other person.

Expressing ideas, motivations, goals, and aims can bring two people closer together than many other activities. And, where there are areas in common – similar interests, ambitions, and plans – this is very thrilling to both partners. The exchange of thoughts and ideas along these lines between a couple who are sexually aware of one another is, in my opinion, one of the most pleasant ways of initiating a sexual relationship, and also it will solidify the relationship once it has begun.

FACIAL EXPRESSIONS AND GESTURES

Another thing to look out for in order to make certain you are sending out the right signals is to keep your facial expressions pleasant. Smiling is especially important since it is a direct way of telling someone that you find him or her attractive. Using hand and head movements are also ways of encouraging people because they indicate interest. Make sure you stand the right distance away – proximity indicates attraction and is a cue for greater intimacy; standing far away points to mistrust and aloofness.

Finally, learning to use touch to communicate can step up the pace of any relationship. To give a positive response in the early stages, touch your partner's arm while talking to him or her or, if you come up from behind, put a hand on his or her shoulder in greeting. Bear in mind that you should keep it subtle. You don't want to overstep the line between showing interest and being too pushy or pawing. Remember, too, that skin-to-skin contact – touching a bare forearm with your finger, for instance – is always much more intimate than skin-to-clothing contact.

When you want to increase the pace further, move on to more prolonged and frequent touching – holding hands, for instance – and from purely social gestures like brushing hands as you pass something to more overtly sexual ones, like lingering pressure on the palm.

JUDGING RESPONSES

By paying attention to body language and other signals, you should be able to see if you are having a positive effect on the other person. Encouraging responses include raised eyebrows, wide-open eyes, and dilated pupils. A definite "come-on" signal is if you are looking into each other's eyes for longer and longer periods, and if you are standing close as you do so. You can test this by moving slightly closer and seeing whether the other person draws away (negative) or not (positive). Watch the gestures the person makes; if he or she nods the head in enthusiastic agreement at what you are saying, or if he or she touches you to emphasize a point when talking to you, you are making progress!

RESPONDING TO AN ADVANCE

Responding to a message requires a lowering of defenses and some risk-taking. Acknowledging that an invitation is being sent to you is one of the riskiest steps. Most of us find ourselves thinking the following: "How well can I trust my senses, even my own ears?" "Have I interpreted the intonation of what is being said correctly; does that person really mean what he or she is saying?" "Why should that person be interested in me?" "Maybe it is just a joke, a tease; will I look like a fool if I take this seriously? But (and it is a big but) will I hate to miss the chance just in case it is serious and I would like to go further?" When an invitation is perceived, all of these thoughts can occur almost simultaneously to the person receiving the advance.

Once an encouraging message is sent, received, and acknowledged, each person is on his or her best behavior and projects the kind of person that they think would please the other. It is only later that partners begin to show their true colors and test how their relationship might work in everyday life with its stresses and strains.

SOME POINTERS FOR MEN

Social responsiveness is not the same as sexual encouragement. And invitations can be misunderstood. For instance, when you're invited to a woman's home for the first time and told to make yourself comfortable, do you remove your jacket, loosen your tie, and lounge on the sofa? Do you allow your anticipation to show and then, when the woman returns in jeans and an old shirt, do you feel like a real fool when she says, "What do you think you're doing, moving in? I have to finish putting up my bookshelves. You can get yourself a drink before letting yourself out."

Nor should you expect every single encounter to lead to great romance or sex. If you get too serious or expect a woman to give you more than she is prepared to, you will probably make her retreat. Many women prefer a softer approach to an overtly sexual come-on, and it is not a good idea to be familiar too soon. Express your admiration and interest, but stay away from endearments or physical caresses at first.

SOME POINTERS FOR WOMEN

Sexual relationships usually progress in small steps, with each of you giving and responding to signs of encouragement. Picking up on and responding to the other's cues correctly will minimize any risk of your social responsiveness being interpreted as sexual encouragement.

It is important, too, to know exactly what you want out of a relationship. Many women are shy about admitting that they just want sex, not a long-term loving relationship. Some women even will go so far as to generate feelings of love in order to have sex, and this, in the long-term, will prove unsatisfactory for both you and your partner.

Do not expect every encounter with a man to lead to great romance or sex. If you get too serious or expect a man to give more than he is prepared to, you will probably make him retreat. It is not usually a good idea to be familiar with him too soon. Express admiration and interest in him, but stay away from endearments or physical caresses during the early stages of the relationship.

AROUSAL

When we are attracted to or aroused by someone sexually, all our senses, but particularly sight, touch, and hearing, come into play. Our sense of smell, while important, plays a much smaller part than it does in other species. Traditionally, it has been the woman who attracts with visual displays of gestures and apparel, and the man who responds with sexual arousal, but changing patterns of sexual behavior have led to a somewhat greater equality of roles. For example, today both sexes wear clothes explicitly to attract the opposite sex – men wear tight pants and form-fitting tops, and women wear low-cut necklines and slim, short skirts.

In terms of the stimuli that excite them, men and women differ markedly. Men, generally, are stimulated by what they see. Women, on the other hand, are very different. As a general rule, they respond very little and very slowly to visual stimuli. Women are more interested in men in the context of their personalities.

WHAT TURNS US ON?

Sight This plays a greater role in arousing men than women, but a woman may take advantage of this by making herself as visually attractive as possible, with a properly made-up face and flattering clothes, and by making sure that her movements – such as when undressing – are pleasing to watch. The eyes are supposed to be the windows of the soul, so it is very common to see lovers gazing intently into each other's eyes, oblivious of everything else around them.

Hearing This contributes much, too, which is why music, played quietly and at the right moment, can be highly exciting for both men and women. We become excited when we hear our beloved approaching, his or her laugh, and particularly his or her voice. Some men and some women have very beautiful voices, and are aware of their seductive effects. A man may have a warm, velvety voice whose every modulation has the power to move a woman's heart. A good voice used well is a caress. A telephone call may simulate an act of love and be as potent as any form of foreplay. The opposite pertains, too, of course, and some voices may literally drive a potential partner mad.

Touch Small touches, even accidental touches, have an enormous effect on everyone. We all need touch very badly. We find it relaxing and reassuring, and it helps us loosen up our inhibitions. Sometimes the greatest intimacy and the most acute closeness can come from simply touching and holding. Most of us have had experiences where dancing has been highly erotic, involving the rhythmical contact of two bodies. Dancing can be pure foreplay – try dancing cheek to cheek, hand in hand, breasts against a man's chest, pelvis against pelvis, legs slightly apart, thighs brushing each other, sexual organs pressed together – all of which simulate sexual contact. The potent mixture of sight and sound created by movement, light, and music only adds to the effect.

Taste A delicious meal accompanied by fine wine often puts a couple in a good mood and lowers their inhibitions so they are more inclined to make love. Talk over a meal, soft lighting, and the ritual of eating can be very seductive, and lovers feel that there is a metaphor between eating and deriving emotional nourishment from a partner's body.

Smell Women like wearing scent and men like smelling it, but it can have a much greater effect than a woman ever thinks – especially when her body is warm; the scent evaporates and body smells mingle with the perfume, acting as a powerful stimulant. Coco Chanel once said that a woman should scent her body wherever she expects to be kissed, and with the array of scents available, both partners would delight in this. Women probably have the strongest preference for the unadulterated smell of a man's skin, which in itself is very exciting, but most wouldn't mind if their partners used some aftershave as a way of showing interest.

——— WHAT MEN LIKE ———

Bare flesh This is rated very highly by men. Exposed bodies and expressions of a "come hither" variety are extremely arousing to most males.

Makeup Bright red lips are a sexual turn-on, as are other things connected with physical appearance, such as hair style and color.

Sexually explicit material Men find "girlie" magazines, soft-porn videos, and pin-up photos very arousing: they use them to feed their fantasies and to enhance masturbation. The majority of men, however, would not be particularly aroused by their own partner appearing in a girlie magazine; it is the fact that such a woman is somebody else's partner that has to do with her attraction.

Sexy clothing Black, lacy underwear and scanty nightclothes are particularly pleasing to most men, hence models posing in suspender belts and stockings.

——— WHAT WOMEN LIKE ———

Physical attractiveness Even though physical appearance is not necessarily at the top of the list of qualities women consider important, most women will confess to being attracted to certain aspects of their partner's body, although not normally their genitals.

Power and wealth Visible evidence of dominance, which is expressed in today's world by being in possession of money and status, are turn-ons for the majority of women.

Romance and intimacy Expressions and manifestations of an intimate or romantic interlude such as champagne, moonlight, and flowers are also arousing to most women.

Erotic literature Although women will confess to enjoyment of erotic literature in the form of romantic novels, sexually explicit material has been found also to excite many women.

THE FIRST SEXUAL EXPERIENCE

The driving force behind your first sexual experience may be love, but it could also be lust, or even curiosity. It is quite usual for most people to be a little apprehensive and tense, and also to feel a little disappointed with the outcome – first-time sex not proving to be the ecstatic experience they might have imagined. Like most things, sex improves with practice and familiarity with a partner. While for most men, orgasm is fairly automatic even on the first occasion, women rarely achieve orgasm with early intercourse; this is something that has to be learned.

MAKING IT BETTER

It will certainly help, however, if you choose the right setting and make sure you have complete privacy with no fear of interruptions. You should decide beforehand whether you will be spending the whole night together or leaving before morning. If the former, you not only need to think about bringing along a change of clothes (and personal toiletry items), but how you feel about waking up in bed with someone you might not know very well.

Allow yourselves plenty of time so that your lovemaking can proceed unhurried, and in a relaxed manner. With the first time this is especially important, since any nervousness that one or both partners feel must be completely dispelled if arousal is to take place. The man particularly should not be in too much of a rush.

Make sure that a reliable form of contraception is used. Lovers should bear in mind, too, that since AIDS and other sexually transmitted diseases – such as genital herpes and chlamydia – can be caught or spread the first time sexual intercourse takes place, the man also should wear a condom (see opposite).

Virgins (both men and women) should declare themselves. This is particularly important for the woman, since she needs to inform her partner to be gentle and not to thrust too deeply at first. The man should always make certain the woman is aroused by caressing and stimulating her for a minimum of ten minutes before penetration. This way she will have enough natural lubrication to make things easier. Saliva or artificial lubricants can also be used to make things more comfortable. Do not use petroleum jelly (such as Vaseline®); it may be irritating to the vagina.

Choose a man-on-top position; putting a pillow beneath the woman's hips also may make it more comfortable for her. Penetration should be gentle but firm, and thrusts should be light. A woman can help her man by guiding his penis into her vagina and bearing down slightly as he enters to relax the pelvic muscles.

SAFE SEX

The notion of "safe sex" was initially promoted in the 1980s as a response to the spread of AIDS, but practicing safe sex will help protect you against sexually transmitted diseases in general and not just against AIDS. Safe sex is a matter of commonsense caution combined with an awareness of the risks involved in different kinds of sexual activity.

High-risk Sexual Activities
• Any sexual act that draws blood, whether intentionally or accidentally.
• Anal intercourse without the use of a condom.
• Vaginal intercourse without the use of a condom.
• Insertion of fingers or a hand into the anus.
• Sharing penetrative sex aids.

Medium-risk Sexual Activities
• Anal intercourse with a condom.
• Vaginal intercourse with a condom.
• Cunnilingus.
• Fellatio, especially to climax.
• Anal kissing or licking.
• Sexual activities involving urination.
• Wet (tongue-to-tongue) kissing.

Low-risk Sexual Activities
• Mutual masturbation (except cunnilingus and fellatio).
• Rubbing of genitals against a partner's body.
• Dry kissing.

No-risk Sexual Activities
• Nongenital massage.
• Self-masturbation.

USING A CONDOM
One of the chief weapons in combating the spread of sexual disease is widespread use of the condom. Although it does not guarantee complete protection, it does reduce the risks substantially.

1 The penis needs to be fully erect and the condom must be in place before vaginal or anal penetration, or oral sex, takes place.

2 Squeeze the teat end free of air and unroll the condom fully over the penis. Do not stretch it tightly or it may burst.

3 During withdrawal, hold the base of the condom to prevent semen from spilling into the vagina. Always use a new condom for each act of intercourse.

INITIATING SEX

While a few individuals believe that one-night stands are one of the most satisfactory forms of human relationships, most people feel that, in addition to physical attraction, there has to be love, and love involves knowing someone intimately. In fact, sex is the ultimate act of knowing. But in order to know someone, you have to show yourself to him or her. For the majority of people knowing is not easy; you feel vulnerable and open to the possibility of being rejected, which can be extremely painful. Sex can rarely be fulfilling without knowing your partner and showing yourself. No relationship can thrive where these two basic ingredients are missing.

Right from the outset, you must tell the truth and nothing but the truth. Any other form of

Becoming intimate
Sex is our primary way of showing love. With a sympathetic, loving, and open partner, it can be a magical voyage of discovery.

behavior is distancing and hypocritical; you must represent yourself honestly. In a loving relationship, even a white lie is an insult and extremely damaging. Honesty in itself is arousing; it can be a stimulant. Truth is probably the best aphrodisiac.

Everyone is vulnerable, both emotionally and romantically, so in a relationship that will involve love and sex, you should declare your vulnerability. Don't forget that having sex is a decision as well as an impulse, and it doesn't mean that you have to lose control. It means letting your partner know that the basic reason for your being there is that you are looking for love; you are looking for someone to bond with. When you decide to have sex with someone, you are being intimate with all he or she is; so declare all you are.

The myth of romanticized women and eroticized men distorts the natural interaction that takes place between the two sexes. The infinite range of human experiences through holding, touching, feeling, stimulating, trusting, talking, and listening to one another is involved in sexual interaction, and it is a distortion of the male and female personality to say that love and sex is the sole prerogative of either gender.

SOME POINTERS FOR MEN

• Take care over your appearance and cleanliness; never fall into bed unshaven and unwashed.

• Have something nice planned; almost all women appreciate thoughtfulness in the form of a bouquet of flowers or a candlelit dinner, for instance.

• Compliment your partner on her appearance, tell her she smells nice, hold her hand, give her light, affectionate kisses, and catch her eye and smile whenever you can.

• Be attentive, whether you're at home, out together, or at a party; for example, don't ignore her for the television.

• Once you're in bed be attentive to her wishes and indulge in as much loving foreplay as you can.

• Try not to fall asleep immediately you've climaxed; talk to her for a while afterward and hold her in your arms.

SOME POINTERS FOR WOMEN

• In matters of love, go for it; don't dissemble and deceive. Nothing works as well as going full tilt after someone you want, and to keep on working at it once you are together. Going after someone means giving yourself.

• Take some care over your appearance; clean, well-cut, sweet-smelling, freely moving hair and an attractively made-up face can be very appealing.

• Be free with your compliments, like telling your partner he's handsome.

• Avoid behaving in an overly critical and unromantic manner, or acting too aggressively about having sex.

• Encourage your partner in his efforts; let him know what you find exciting in nice ways that will please him.

• Sexy underwear, subtle perfume, and a readiness to cuddle and be close can all be terrific come-ons.

YOUR APPEARANCE

While there may be many ways of enjoying sex, most people will enjoy sex more if they are sure of themselves – not simply sure of what they are doing, but sure of their attractiveness and desirability.

Attractiveness or sex appeal is hard to define, but sexuality has more to do with your attitude toward yourself, your partner, and your lifestyle than with anything else, and certainly more than with obvious physical attributes. We have all met rather plain, unassuming people who have great charm and attraction, which is difficult to pin down but often has to do with having a positive attitude toward life, a ready smile, a subtle sense of humor, and enthusiasm. Other people are attractive because of their eccentricity and uniqueness – how they speak or express themselves, mannerisms, surprising candor, or individualistic presentation.

Such qualities are probably more important than your actual appearance, and while it is worth spending some time on how you look, you should maintain a sense of balance by not becoming obsessive about your physical appearance. Too many men and women feel dissatisfied because they compare themselves to an exaggerated image of what is good-looking. Responding to your partner and being willing to share pleasure are the qualities that ultimately make a person attractive.

Although overattention to appearance is not necessary, some relationships can founder if either partner neglects his or her appearance and hygiene. The best possible reason for taking trouble over your appearance is for your own self-esteem, but you should also do so for the sake of your partner, otherwise he or she could interpret neglect as a sign of not caring. This does not imply that one has to spend hours on preparation, but an unclean and/or smelly body, dowdy, ill-kempt clothes, an unshaven face, curlers in the hair, and an ill-tempered face all imprint themselves on the memory and become difficult to erase at times of intimacy. A sloppy appearance invites comparison with the time when you first met, and the inevitable thought arises that love is on the wane.

LOOKING AT YOURSELF POSITIVELY

Many people find it worthwhile to take a good, hard look at themselves as a way of getting in touch with and appreciating their bodies. Most of us are far too hard on ourselves. It will buck up your feelings quite a lot if you concentrate on your good points rather than emphasizing the bad.

Doing the following should help to lessen self-consciousness and make you more comfortable with yourself and your body as a source of sexual pleasure. It is best to do these "exercises" in private, when you have plenty of time and feel as relaxed as possible.

MAN'S SELF-APPRAISAL

1 Undress and stand in front of a full-length mirror. Examine your naked body carefully, from head to toe. Imagine you are seeing yourself for the first time. Look at yourself from every angle.

2 Stand, kneel, bend, and then move around. Sit with your legs apart and then together. Look over your shoulder to see the curve of your back and the set of your buttocks.

3 Focus attention on your best points; everybody has some. They might be the breadth of your chest, the flatness of your stomach, the fullness of your hair, or your height.

4 Then pay attention to the features that you dislike and try to see them in a more positive way. For instance, while you may think yourself shorter than you would like, you may be trim and perfectly proportioned.

5 Now study your genitals. Feel your testes; one, usually the left, will hang slightly below the other. Your flaccid penis will probably be between 2 and 4 inches (5 and 10 centimeters) long and, when you touch it, you will find the most sensitive area is the head and, in particular, the ridge on the underside.

6 Finish by taking a warm bath. Soap your hands and explore your body with them, noticing all the different sensations you experience by changes in touch and pressure. Explore your penis and testicles again, too, if you like, but try to become aware of sensations throughout your whole body.

WOMAN'S SELF-APPRAISAL

1 Stand naked in front of a full-length mirror and take the time to examine your body carefully, from head to toe as though you were seeing yourself for the first time. Use another mirror to see yourself from the side or back.

2 Move around. Kneel, bend, and sit with your legs apart, then together.

3 Concentrate on your best points; you are bound to have some. The shapeliness of your legs, the length of your neck, high cheekbones, or dainty feet, for example.

4 Reconsider the features that you dislike and try to see them in a more positive light. For instance, although you may think that you are fatter than the ideal, you may have a Rubenesque physique that is attractive to men.

5 Using a hand mirror, and in the best possible light, examine your vagina. Identify your different parts. In order to see and touch the clitoris properly, you will need to pull back the hood of skin covering it. You can run your fingers along the inner and outer vaginal lips and back along the area between the anus and vagina to find the more sensitive areas. Separate the inner lips in order to explore the entrance to the vagina and inside.

6 When you have finished, take a warm bath. Soap your hands and explore your body with them, noticing the different sensations you experience in all your body areas by changes in touch and pressure.

THE SEXUAL REPERTOIRE

The activities described here are practiced by most people. Some more bizarre practices, which occur rarely and may not be embraced whole-heartedly by both partners, haven't been included. Your sexual experience may include some or all of the activities listed below; if the former, you might like to try out the new ones. Remember that for truly satisfying experiences, partners must learn how to receive as well as give.

— WHAT MEN CAN DO —

• You talk warmly or sexually to your partner to arouse her.
• You hold or rub your body against your partner's body.
• You kiss your partner passionately.
• You kiss with your tongues in each other's mouths.
• You fondle your partner's body when she is clothed.
• You undress your partner and see her naked body.
• You caress your partner's naked body.
• You kiss your partner's breasts and lick, suck, or gently take her nipples into your mouth.
• With your hands you explore and stroke your partner's vaginal area.
• You lick and kiss around and inside your partner's vagina.
• You bring your partner to orgasm by stimulating her clitoris and vaginal area with your hands and fingers.
• You bring your partner to orgasm by stimulating her clitoris and vaginal area with your mouth.
• You reach orgasm by intercourse in any of the following positions: with you on top; lying side-by-side; with you approaching behind; with your partner on top; both sitting; both kneeling; both standing.
• You fondle or kiss your partner's buttocks and anal area.

— WHAT WOMEN CAN DO —

• You use sexual terms in your conversation and speak intimately to your partner.
• You take your partner's body and hold it or rub it against yours.
• You offer him a variety of kisses.
• You engage in open-mouthed kissing, with your tongues inside each other's mouths.
• While he is clothed, you fondle your partner's body.
• You take off your partner's clothes and look at his naked body.
• On your partner's naked body, you bestow a variety of caresses.
• You lick or gently suck your partner's nipples.
• Using your hands, you explore and stroke your partner's penis and testicles.
• You lick and kiss your partner's penis and testicles.
• While stimulating his penis with your hands, you enable your partner to reach orgasm.
• Using your mouth on his penis, you bring your partner to orgasm.
• You reach orgasm by intercourse in the following positions: your partner on top; lying side-by-side; with you on top; with your partner approaching from behind; sitting; kneeling; standing.
• You caress or kiss your partner's buttocks and anus.

FOREPLAY

Satisfying lovemaking takes time and can never take too long. On rare occasions, you may become so aroused during foreplay that you immediately move on to actual intercourse, but usually a couple enjoys the gradual intimacies that leisurely kissing, undressing, petting, massage, oral sex, and the sharing of fantasies – among others – provide. Foreplay should be savored as an integral part of lovemaking. Learn to excite each other slowly but surely, discovering and exploring your partner's erogenous zones and whole body in a loving, caring, thoughtful, and not simply mechanical, way, so that lovemaking becomes a truly shared experience.

BECOMING AROUSED

Satisfying lovemaking takes time and can never take too long. There are numerous activities for lovers to indulge in that do not involve actual sexual intercourse. On rare occasions, you may be so aroused that you immediately proceed to penetration and an orgasm, but usually a couple enjoys the gradual intimacies that leisurely kissing, undressing, petting, and oral sex, among others, provide.

The variety of techniques that can be used to please each other can be enjoyed as activities in their own right, or as delightful prologues to sexual intercourse. The longer, more refined, and attentive the foreplay is, the more receptive you and your body will become, and the better, more magical, and more fulfilling the ultimate pleasure will be.

A MAN'S NEED FOR FOREPLAY

Contrary to popular belief, men too need and enjoy foreplay. It offers them the necessary stimulation to build up a good, firm erection and prepare the penis for intercourse. In fact, numerous cases of impotence could be prevented if foreplay was long and exciting enough.

There are, however, a few situations where the length and type of foreplay need to be carefully discussed, and that is where a man experiences premature ejaculation or where he has trouble maintaining an erection. In those cases, if he is undergoing therapy, he may want to keep foreplay to a minimum.

Some men see foreplay as a variety of things they have to go through in order to prepare their partners for intercourse. Others want their partners to touch their genitals immediately. Encourage your man to appreciate the delights foreplay offers by being enthusiastic about trying new sensual experiences so that he learns that joy in sexual activities comes in a large part from the affection expressed between you.

A WOMAN'S NEED FOR FOREPLAY

A woman's body requires prolonged stimulation if she is to become fully aroused. Arousal is brought on by a complex blend of mental and physical stimuli when the emotional atmosphere is sufficiently encouraging.

Some women need a particularly long time, and a considerate lover must therefore be patient. As you arouse your partner, you will feel intense pleasure as well, and she will not only be more receptive but also more helpful during intercourse, so that the experience will be equally pleasurable for both of you. Men who kiss and cuddle a lot, and indulge in sensitive foreplay, are much more likely to see their partners reach orgasm frequently and easily.

Don't be in a hurry to undress your partner and proceed immediately to touching her breasts and vagina. Hold her close, and keep early caresses non-genital. Concentrate on your partner. Let the resulting feelings range all over your body, and avoid thinking solely about what is happening to your penis.

UNDRESSING

Removing your clothes, and/or those of your partner, can be a very exciting and important part of foreplay. Undressing not only results in general arousal but the wearing of and/or removal of particular items of clothing can strike a much more resonant chord in a susceptible lover, particularly a man.

A good lover will seek to discover which garments and their removal will act as turn-ons, and will make use of them to increase a partner's pleasure. You may have to practice removing your partner's clothes with one hand, and without clumsiness or delays, if undressing is to be a truly exciting aspect of foreplay.

Nudity may become routine and boring, particularly in marriage, so some subtlety in undressing is worth retaining. Even after years of living together, undressing each other will be highly arousing; each partner should feel increasingly excited as one garment after another is removed.

WHAT A MAN FINDS EXCITING

Many men prefer a hint of nudity to total nudity since it lets the imagination run riot. Lovely, lacy, fine lingerie is attractive to and exciting for men, both the sight of it and its removal. Your man may well enjoy making love particularly when you keep on an undergarment such as a slip, stockings, garter belt, panties, bra, or camisole.

The removal of certain clothes, especially garments that emphasize a woman's breasts, buttocks, and genitals, is almost universally a turn-on. Women who take time about getting undressed, and who "accidentally" reveal parts of themselves, are certain to excite their men. If a woman strips off in front of her partner, this active display of herself has an impact that no man can fail to find erotic. The memory of his partner undressing may prove irresistible, and he will want to recreate this scene over and over again in his mind.

WHAT A WOMAN FINDS EXCITING

Wearing lovely, lacy, fine lingerie is attractive to and exciting for women. Many like to retain an undergarment such as a slip, stockings, garter belt, panties, bra, or camisole during the early stages of foreplay. Many women also like their men occasionally to retain some of their garments during sex, though not their socks. A hint of nudity allows the imagination to run riot.

A lot of women prefer to have their partners undress them because it allows them to show off their bodies passively without being sexually overt. Other women may feel sufficiently confident to strip in front of their partners. If done with artistry (something that may require a bit of enjoyable practice in front of a mirror), it will be highly erotic, mainly because the woman's role is no longer passive. She is actively displaying herself in an attempt to arouse her partner, and he knows this.

KISSING

A kiss is very often the first expression of love, and no matter in what other sexual activities a person may indulge, kissing remains one of the most voluptuous of all caresses. The mouth is highly responsive and mobile, and can offer a great variety of sensual pleasures. Through it you are able to experience touch and taste at the same time.

Kisses can be tender, light, and lingering or passionate, deep, burning, and even rough. Between couples who are strongly attracted to one another, kissing can mimic intercourse; the tongue penetrates the mouth with the same rhythmical intensity of the penis in the woman's body.

There is an infinite variety to kisses, with lips closed or open, dry or moist, still or moving, explorative or quietly tender. What lends variety to kissing, too, is that it can be done to any part of the body. It should not be restricted to mouth-to-mouth contact; kissing should be used on every crease and in every crevice. Kissing your lover's erogenous zones, particularly the genital parts, can be the most intimate and stimulating part of foreplay, and here kisses can result in the most profound reactions. For some people, kissing is a necessary accompaniment to orgasm and lends passion and depth to their climaxes.

Heightened sexual response
A kiss can be highly arousing.
A woman can feel it
in the breasts and
genital area, and
often by itself, it
can result in
orgasm.

—— WHAT A MAN LIKES ——

Although the notion persists in a few men that kissing may be "soft," the vast majority enjoy the physical closeness and body contact that it brings. Few men, however, would be content to stop at kissing, especially if there was any possibility of intercourse, and often kisses that a woman means to be simply affectionate, without further promise, can be misunderstood as an invitation to greater intimacy.

Men love to be kissed passionately, and you will be almost certain to arouse your partner by kissing and caressing certain areas such as the back of his neck, his ears, and eyelids. Use deep, sensuous kisses to stimulate his lips, tongue, and the inside of his mouth. Flick your tongue in and out of his mouth and try to have your tongues touching.

Gentle biting and nibbling can be highly erotic as well, but it's best to avoid "love bites" on the genitals, which are highly sensitive and may be easily damaged or caused excessive pain. While some men particularly enjoy having their nipples kissed, nibbled, licked, and sucked, what most men love above all is having their penises kissed (see also Performing Fellatio, p. 60).

—WHAT A WOMAN LIKES —

Women enjoy kissing very much, and most complain that they don't get enough of it – too many men proceed to genital touching far too soon. Women enjoy a rather gradual progression to the genitals, and like having their ears, necks, shoulders, breasts, stomachs, inner thighs, knees, and feet kissed along the way. Women also use kissing as a way of initiating sex and stimulating interest in their partners.

Simple kisses on the lips can be quite delicious, but many women enjoy deep tongue-to-tongue kisses and hard, prolonged kisses on the lips. You will be almost certain to arouse your partner by kissing and caressing certain areas such as the back of her neck, her hair, ears, cheeks, and eyelids. Use deep, sensuous kisses to stimulate your partner's lips and tongue and the inside of her mouth. Tantalize her by flicking your tongue in and out of her mouth and try to have your tongues touching.

Gentle biting and nibbling can be highly erotic as well, but it's best to avoid "love bites" on the genitals, which are highly sensitive and may be damaged or caused excessive pain, and on the breasts, where gentle sucking is more widely preferred. Some women can even reach orgasm this way. And for many women, kissing can be an end in itself.

EROGENOUS ZONES

Discovering and exploring your partner's erogenous zones should be loving, caring, and thoughtful, not simply mechanical. Every woman should try to discover as much as possible about her man's body, and every man should experiment to find out what exactly will please his partner. Couples should learn to excite each other slowly but surely, and gradually find out which parts of the body will provide the most pleasure and stimulation when touched.

As you kiss and stroke various parts of your partner's body, he or she should always let you know immediately what effect your touch has, and you should always express the rising excitement that you feel. Mutual feedback is necessary for successful lovemaking.

For both men and women, stimulation of the erogenous zones begins with the hands and fingers but, of course, all these areas respond even more intensely to touches from the mouth, lips, and tongue. In addition to gentle stroking, patting, and rubbing, occasional gentle slaps should be used to bring variety to sensation and lovemaking techniques. Men will also enjoy their partners using their breasts and nipples to caress them; women find the most potent touch is from the penis, particularly the glans penis, which to them is a miracle of softness and hardness.

DISCOVERING A MAN'S EROGENOUS ZONES

In common with those erogenous zones enjoyed by women such as the lips, any area of the face, and the fingertips, there are certain general areas of a man's body that are very pleasurable for him when touched, for instance, the shoulders, the palms of the hands, the back, the chest, and the nipples. Stroking and sucking your partner's nipples gives pleasure, and they will become erect, a sign of arousal.

A man's entire genital area responds to the slightest touch; within this area there are many specific points to be explored. The area just behind the root of the penis, between the penis and the anus that overlies the prostate gland, can be exceptionally sensitive to touch, both in arousal and in reaching orgasm. The

testes are very sensitive and must be handled gently, as excessive or clumsy handling can hurt. Unquestionably, the penis is a man's most sensitive erogenous zone and the place where he experiences the most intense feelings. The whole shaft of the penis is very sensitive but the glans at the tip is particularly rich in nerve endings, especially on its crown. The frenulum is also extremely sensitive in all men, as is the area lying just behind the opening.

The buttocks are a sexually arousable area; most men find pleasure in having their buttocks caressed, and some men also like having them gently slapped or spanked. The anus is also very sensitive to caresses of all types.

DISCOVERING A WOMAN'S EROGENOUS ZONES

In contrast to a man, all of a woman's skin is an erogenous zone and all of it will respond to touches, caresses, and kisses. However, there are certain areas where stimulation results in more intense arousal. These erogenous zones vary from woman to woman.

GENERAL BODY AREAS

A woman's face has several erogenous zones including her hairline, forehead, temples, eyebrows, eyelids, and cheeks. In general, women prefer light facial caresses. The mouth for most women is one of their most sensitive zones, and it can be stimulated readily with the fingertips and kisses. Stimulating a woman's mouth can set her whole body on fire, and has a direct effect on arousing her genital organs. On the other hand, erogenous stimulation of any other part of a woman's body often produces a reaction in her mouth, in her breasts, and in her genital organs as well.

The earlobes are extremely sensitive to stimulation and can be caressed gently; some women can even have an orgasm after such a simple caress. The neck, particularly at the back and down the sides, is a very sensitive area. The arms, armpits, hands, back, hips, and the whole of the lower abdomen can also be stimulated erotically.

An extremely sensitive zone is the area around the navel. Most women relish caresses with the fingertips, lips, or penis over the whole length of their legs, particularly on the inner thighs.

THE MOST RESPONSIVE SITES

For most women the breasts are highly erotic and play a vital part in sexual excitement. Sucking, nibbling, licking, stroking, and gentle squeezing will cause the nipples to become erect, a certain sign of arousal. However, women do differ greatly here in their reactions to stimulation, so it's important to find out exactly what she likes and doesn't like.

The most highly erogenous area of a woman's body includes the perineum, an area of skin between the vagina and the anus. If you put your whole hand on this area, with the outer lips of the vagina closed, and press hard or massage, a woman can be aroused extremely quickly because of the dense network of nerve endings.

Both the inner and outer lips of the perineal area are extremely rich in nerve endings also, and are a highly erogenous zone. The inner lips, however, are much more sensitive than the outer ones, especially if stroked along their inner surfaces along the cleft of the vulva. If you press both lips together and firmly massage with your fingers all the sensitive parts of the vulva, high levels of excitement should result. The clitoris is the most sexually sensitive part of a woman's body, and the easiest part to stimulate if a man can learn to do it gently and skillfully, without haste. Stimulation of the clitoris with the tip of the erect penis is particularly pleasurable to many women.

As with the mouth, the entrance to the vagina is rich in nerve endings and reacts intensely to all sorts of caresses (the ultimate being from the glans of the penis), but it can be ecstatic for some women to be caressed there by a man's lips and his tongue.

The buttocks are another erogenous zone and they are easily stimulated by patting, rubbing, or gentle slaps.

PETTING

Whether sexual intercourse is on the agenda or not, a man's generalized kissing and cuddling will sooner or later lead to his touching, caressing, and kissing a woman's breasts, nipples, and clitoris, and a woman will be encouraged to do the same to a man's scrotum and penis. Petting, or love play using fingers, is more than just romantic. It is vital to the escalating spiral of sexual excitement necessary for satisfying sexual intercourse.

WHAT A MAN LIKES

Kissing should lead into and blend with caresses over the man's whole body. Passionate kissing, sucking, and stroking are all pleasurable. Vivid sensations can be produced in a man, too, by slowly and seductively rubbing your hands or other body parts on his bare skin.

Men are easily aroused by having their genitals stimulated (although it is in a woman's interest to prolong foreplay and delay genital caressing until nearer to penetration), and many men also enjoy having their buttocks stroked, kneaded, or smacked. Many men also take great pleasure in having their scrotums and testes held or squeezed. The crescendo reached in such ascending sexual activity can frequently bring a man to orgasm without penetrative sex taking place.

Petting is extremely powerful. Sexual excitement begins with some stimulus that orders the pituitary gland in the brain to send out a hormone that travels through the bloodstream in order to stimulate the testes into releasing more hormone, and this makes a man feel sexy and aroused. The hormones themselves push the hypothalamus into producing more of its hormone. This process is an escalating spiral in which the sexier a man feels, the more sexy he will be. It is in a woman's interest to maintain this high level of arousal.

WHAT A WOMAN LIKES

One of the reasons why petting is so potent and so enjoyed by women is that it arouses and prepares them for sexual intercourse. For women, intercourse is welcome only when they have had enough stimulation so that the vagina lubricates and unfolds, ready to receive the penis. Without the chance to build up the level of sex hormones through kissing, caressing, and petting, intercourse can be very uncomfortable for a woman. Most men underestimate how long this takes, since their own erections occur much more quickly.

Kissing should lead into and blend with caresses all over a woman's body. Most women prefer initial caresses to be in areas other than the breasts and genitals, but once they have begun to feel aroused, they do enjoy having their breasts and bottoms stimulated. Breasts, however, need careful stroking until a woman is more highly aroused, then more passionate kissing, sucking, and stroking are pleasurable. Most women like their buttocks caressed or squeezed; some enjoy gentle smacking. Only when a woman is sufficiently aroused does she want her partner to move on to genital caresses. Women differ in their tastes, but most prefer initial genital caresses to be gentle, with harder, more vigorous movements as they approach orgasm.

MASSAGE

Mastering the techniques of sexual and nonsexual touching is very important to a satisfactory sexual relationship. For people who already enjoy a good sex life, massage can enhance enjoyment; for most of us, there is plenty of room for improvement.

Massage is important not only because it has the general effect of relaxing you and giving you the chance to really think about and enjoy touching but it also allows you to focus your senses acutely and deeply on the responses that are aroused in your body, and in this way increases your sex drive. During massage some people experience this "sensate focusing" for the very first time.

Massage can be particularly important for women because it can have exactly the same effect as kissing, caressing, and other forms of foreplay, in that it allows a woman's sex hormones to build up and to arouse and prepare her body for intercourse. It is helpful also for men who have difficulty in arousal or suffer from impotence.

One of the aims of massage is to give you the opportunity to discover for yourself what gives you pleasure, and you should approach it with a completely open mind. Men and women are often surprised how sexy it feels to have certain parts of their bodies – which they had never thought of as remotely erotic – caressed.

GETTING THE MAXIMUM PLEASURE

Getting to know every inch of your lover's body is among the most pleasurable shared experiences, and it is worth taking the time and trouble to set the scene properly. You should alternate between being the passive or pleasure-giving partner. Choose a time when you won't be interrupted, and a place that is warm and private. Soft lighting and background music also can contribute. You can use a bed that isn't too soft, or the floor with sufficient cushions.

Both partners should adopt comfortable positions and should be undressed to get the maximum benefit. The person giving the massage should make certain his or her hands are warm and preferably oiled. If you are the pleasure-giving partner, concentrate on what you are doing and how your partner is responding. If it is your turn to be on the receiving end, lie back and enjoy every minute.

Start with a gentle, exploratory massage, going over all parts of your partner's body except the genitals and breasts, since this will make the process much more sensual and relaxed. You can, if you like, of course, go on to touching the breasts and genitals, and this may prove so arousing that sexual intercourse or an orgasm cannot be avoided.

MASTURBATION

The majority of both men and women come to know about their own sexuality through masturbation, which usually starts around age 10 or 11. Of course, boys and girls do play with themselves long before this, particularly boys, who may grasp their penises in their first year of life, but only because it is an appendage that juts out from their body.

As a pleasurable sensation, although not a sexual one, toddlers fondle themselves around the ages of three and four, and may explore each other around the ages of five and six, but it is not until adolescence, when sex hormones are being produced, that masturbation for sexual pleasure starts. Age 10 or 11 is the earliest, but it can start much later. For some, masturbation is not experienced until the late teens or early 20s.

It is only through personal experimentation that people come to understand their preferences and develop techniques that they find most pleasing. But it is essential that these preferences are expressed to a partner, and that the techniques are candidly shared.

In the majority of people, autoerotic experience is highly private and masturbation is one of the most difficult of all topics for couples to discuss. Perhaps religious orientation forbids it, or it still may be an area they feel unable to discuss because it is so highly private. Many people find masturbation a difficult subject to approach because they think they have to share what they actually do. This isn't at all necessary, but you should try to share with your partner how you feel.

Autoerotism, of course, is not limited to self-stimulation of the genital organs; there are many other experiences in life that are autoerotic, such as taking a long, luxurious, sensuous bath, or simply feeling the wind in your hair and the sun on your skin. Don't limit your view of autoerotism entirely to sex; allow yourself to be stimulated by the many naturally occurring, everyday experiences such as a crisp, sunny winter morning, a walk along the beach on a fine day, or swimming in the ocean.

ATTITUDES TOWARD MASTURBATION

Many women think of masturbation as unnatural and disgusting and a complete waste of time. They don't understand why anybody does it, and they are unsympathetic to the view that people might continue to do it even though they have sexual partners. The majority of men, although they may keep their feelings to themselves, don't agree.

For most people, once it is faced, masturbation in front of, or with a partner, particularly if it is mutual, can be an extremely enjoyable and exciting way of making love, especially if it comes at the end of an extended period of foreplay. Differences in attitudes can be ironed out only if you are candid with your partner and voice your feelings about masturbation. You may get a shock; you may find that you are both mutually attracted to the idea.

There are many myths about masturbation, but it is important to realize that masturbation cannot cause any trouble for anyone unless it is against one's own moral sanctions. View it as an excellent opportunity for self-education. You should be open and comfortable with it; it should never end up leaving impressions of hurriedness, guilt, or secretiveness about sex. More importantly, masturbation can lead to intense orgasms, and it is the one way to develop sexual comfort, security, and self-esteem.

Above all, engaging in masturbation does not mean that sex with your partner is not as good as it should be, or even that your partner cannot stimulate your genital organs in the way that you like. Many partners have their best sexual experiences when masturbation or mutual masturbation is engaged in prior to or during sexual intercourse.

WHAT A MAN LIKES

Male masturbation has always been a secret from which women have been excluded. Even in marriage, few women are given the opportunity to witness it. But without knowledge of how your partner gives himself pleasure, it is difficult for you to know how to. There is no better way to learn about what he likes than to look and talk.

A man's sexual focus is the head of his penis; this is in contrast to women who have a far greater range of sensation-producing apparatus. (In addition to the high level of response concentrated on the clitoral shaft and glans, women can be excited by stimulation of the labia, the opening into the vagina, and the vagina itself.) Touching the scrotal sac and the testes is not as exciting for men as stimulation of the labial area or the vaginal entrance is for women.

A man concentrates his efforts on the glans and frenulum. The shaft is relatively insensitive and allows him to move his hand up and down rhythmically.

WHAT A WOMAN LIKES

The easiest way for a man to find out how a woman likes to be stimulated, and how much stimulation is necessary, is to study how women masturbate. Some women, however, especially those who may have guilty feelings about self-pleasure, prefer to be masturbated by their partners. Many women do it at particular times, such as while they are menstruating, and keep it secret from their partners. Others may indulge in it routinely as a way of relieving sexual tension. Because direct and continued genital stimulation is so necessary to a woman's orgasm, some women use masturbation as a way of guaranteeing that they reach a climax while having sexual intercourse.

In fact, since only about 30 percent of women achieve orgasm with intercourse but over 80 percent experience a climax with masturbation, orgasm by means of masturbation, rather than by sexual intercourse, should be regarded as the normal experience.

MASTURBATION CAN BE FUN

Masturbation is an option, a way of mutually enhancing a couple's sexual enjoyment. Masturbation is generally helpful to sexuality in all areas of your life. That doesn't mean that if you don't masturbate you're abnormal; you're not inadequate or deficient.

Remember that masturbation does not reflect badly on your sexual activity; in fact, there is some evidence showing that people who masturbate without guilt are freer in expressing their sexuality, more aware of the nature of their own sexual response, and therefore enjoy sex more than those who are guilt-ridden. Moreover, masturbation is a good alternative to intercourse for women in late pregnancy or just after childbirth, or following gynecological surgery; also, when a man can't get an erection.

CAN A MAN MASTURBATE TOO MUCH?

Men commonly report masturbatory frequency ranging from once a month to two or three times a day. Nearly every man is concerned about the supposed mental effects of excessive masturbation, but does not consider his own level to be excessive. A man who masturbates once a month sees once or twice a week as excessive, with mental illness as a quite possible complication of such frequency. A man who masturbates two or three times a day thinks five or six times a day is excessive. No man, however, has the fear that his particular masturbatory pattern is excessive, regardless of frequency.

There is no medical evidence to suggest that masturbation, regardless of frequency, leads to any form of mental illness. In fact, it may be the case that men masturbate too little – both in time spent and in number of occasions. More pleasure, more sensuality, and greater control can be positive results of masturbatory activity.

CAN A WOMAN MASTURBATE TOO MUCH?

For most women, masturbation is the introduction to sex. Few women have a clear idea of their own sexual anatomy, so they wouldn't know where they like stimulation unless they'd masturbated. Masturbation helps a girl to know how she functions sexually, and it helps her form preferences. It may even give her the first orgasm.

Women can often find it harder than men to achieve orgasm, and the ability to discover what feels good and exciting, what arouses them and what makes them less inhibited, less fearful and more willing to let go is most often discovered through masturbation. Once a woman has achieved orgasm by this means, it becomes easier to repeat.

Masturbation is important for older women too. It increases lubrication and reduces vaginal pain due to dryness. Whether it has been continual, or taken up again on the loss of a partner, it is an ideal sexual activity – an easy way of achieving orgasm – and one guaranteed to prolong your sexually active life.

WHAT MEN DO

It is only through experimentation that each man discovers how best he likes to be stimulated. Some men use only the lightest of touches on the upper surface of the penis; some use strong, gripping, and stroking movements over the whole organ that for many other individuals could be painful. Often, men prefer to stimulate the glans alone; they either confine their manipulation to the upper surface of the penis on or close to the frenulum, or pull to stimulate the entire area of the glans. Most men, however, manipulate the penile shaft with stroking movements that encompass the entire organ; rapidity, length of movement, and tightness vary from man to man.

Many men masturbate incorrectly; they try to get it done as quickly as possible and much of their technique and timing is wrong. This may result in problems later, since many men come to associate masturbation and ejaculation with getting rid of tension quickly.

As ejaculation approaches, most men increase their actions until they are stroking the penile shaft as rapidly as possible. During ejaculation, most men either ease completely or markedly slow the movements along the shaft. This is because the glans is quite sensitive right after ejaculation. (This is something rarely appreciated by women, who often have very different preferences, see right.) It can be distressing for a man if a woman continues to carry out active manual stroking or pelvic thrusting immediately subsequent to ejaculation.

Some men find using a lubricant on their hands can enhance their pleasure. Petroleum jelly, hand or body lotions, and massage oils can all make the experience more pleasurable.

WHAT WOMEN DO

No two women masturbate in the same way, although they rarely manipulate the glans of the clitoris directly, since it often becomes overly sensitive to touch or pressure. This is particularly the case immediately after orgasm, and care must be taken to avoid direct contact with the glans unless renewed stimulation is desired. Some women move their bodies to feel sensuous, others lie quite still and let only their hands work.

Most women who manipulate the clitoris do this through the shaft, manipulating the right side if right-handed, and vice versa. Many women change sides; concentrated manipulation can give rise to numbness if too much pressure is applied to any one area.

Very few women concentrate on the clitoris itself; most stimulate the mons area in general. Indeed, the entire perineal area becomes highly sensitive to touch; the labia minora may also be a main source of erotic arousal.

During masturbation, most women manipulate the shaft of the clitoris continuously right up to orgasm and through it without a break. This is the opposite of the usual man's reaction to orgasm, which is to stop rapid pelvic thrusting; stopping clitoral stimulation can account for the lack of a satisfactory orgasm in females during intercourse. Unlike a man, a woman who masturbates often is not content with a single orgasm but may well enjoy several subsequent orgasms until fatigue intervenes.

Some masturbation techniques, such as rolling on an object or climaxing by clenching the perineal muscles, are difficult to integrate with intercourse, and a woman may need to adjust her practices when a partner is involved.

STIMULATING A WOMAN

To provide the most satisfying sensations over the entire clitoral area, use the whole hand – all the fingers, palm or the heel of the hand – rather than just one or two fingers. Your fingers need to be well lubricated so use vaginal fluid, saliva, or jellies (see p. 63). There are two major types of movement, circular and vibratory.

For circular movements, place your hand over the clitoral area. Apply light pressure with your palm or fingers, moving them gently around and around.

Move your hand up so that the heel is right over the clitoris at the top of the vulva and is resting partly on the pubic bone on either side, where you can press firmly as you rub.

Alternatively, you can press gently with your hand, palm downward over the pubic mound so that your fingers overhang the clitoris, and make firm, circular movements.

For vibratory movements, cup your hand over the pubic area and vibrate it rapidly, brushing your fingers to and fro across the clitoris. Then, keeping your hand still, put a finger on each side of the vaginal lips and vibrate them from side to side. Pressing firmly through the fleshy folds, rub on each side of the inner vaginal lips at the base of the clitoris.

Most women also often enjoy being penetrated by a finger while their clitoris is being stimulated. Make sure that your fingernail is short and straight before slipping your middle finger into the vagina, keeping your other fingers bent forward so that the knuckles continue to press against the clitoris. You can move your finger in and out gently, applying pressure on the front wall of the vagina. Alternatively, rub the tip of your penis against the clitoris.

HOW TO STIMULATE A WOMAN
The clitoris is delicate and highly sensitive; most women find indirect pressure more comfortable than direct pressure.

1 Placing your hand over your partner's entire perineum or vaginal area, while applying light pressure and gentle circular movements will increase her arousal.

2 When your partner is sufficiently lubricated, insert your finger into her vagina and move it gently in and out, while keeping contact with the clitoris.

STIMULATING A MAN

To be a good lover, knowing how to stimulate the penis is one of the most valuable skills that a woman can possess. Older men especially may need direct stimulation to reach erection, but men of all ages enjoy the sensations they receive from manipulation. You can use these techniques both as an adjunct to, or as a replacement for intercourse, and vary your approach as much as you like, such as rolling the penis between your palms, stroking it with your fingers, alternately squeezing and letting it go, brushing your fingertips against the frenulum, or caressing the penis between your breasts. To enhance his sensations, and especially if your partner has erection difficulties, use a lubricant (see p. 63).

To begin, position yourself beside your partner. With your thumb nearest his navel, grip his penis firmly. Move your hand up and down on the penis in a regular rhythm, keeping your grip steady and the firmest pressure on the sensitive area on the uppermost side. Try long and short strokes to see what he likes best. A slow rhythm prolongs pleasure, while an accelerated one intensifies pleasure and will bring him to orgasm sooner.

Your partner's climax is imminent when his muscles, particularly those in his thighs, tense up and his breathing gets more rapid. The testes will be drawn up to his body and may also be swollen. The head of the penis will darken in color and increase slightly in size. One or two drops of preejaculatory fluid may ooze from the tip of his penis.

Your partner will want you to carry on with the stimulation until ejaculation is completely over and his tension relaxes. Most men will want you to desist from further genital caresses for a while.

HOW TO STIMULATE A MAN
All men find genital caresses highly stimulating; however, after ejaculation most prefer the stroking to cease.

1 Hold the penis close to the head to ensure optimum stimulation of the underside of the penis, as well as the glans and frenulum.

2 Your partner may want to control the rhythm. With his hand over yours, grasp the penis firmly, though gently, and move your hand rhythmically up and down the shaft, either quickly or slowly according to what your partner wishes.

57

ORAL SEX

Fellatio, sucking, or otherwise stimulating a penis with the mouth, with or without ejaculation, is almost always the most powerful way of arousing a man, and all find it intensely exciting.

The mouth appears to men as similar to, but more exciting than, a vagina, particularly because the tongue is actively used to stimulate. In fact, the mouth is exceptionally well designed for sexual pleasure and is capable of a broad range of activities such as stroking, kissing, licking, probing, and penetrating. The mouth is also the recipient of a wide variety of sensations including the many tastes of a lover's body parts.

Cunnilingus, using the tongue and mouth to lick and nuzzle the clitoris and vaginal area, is highly arousing to a great many women. The tongue is softer than the fingers so it provides gentler and more varied stimulation. Most men are willing, if not always enthusiastic, to perform cunnilingus on their partners.

There is no doubt that oral sex is an intensely intimate experience and that it demands a level of trust that is rarely found in other areas of lovemaking; for one thing, the act can be extremely painful if care isn't taken. This intimacy generally contributes to the participants' satisfaction since it implies total acceptance of each other. To some people, it is the ultimate expression of love.

MAKING IT FUN

A woman's fear of ejaculate in the mouth will be minimized if partners agree beforehand on what is to be done. If ejaculation in the mouth is to be avoided, the man should signal and withdraw in time so that his partner can continue with manual stimulation. Fear of choking is easily dealt with by the woman controlling how much of the penis she takes into her mouth, or by encircling the base of the penis with her hand to hold back his thrusting.

Worry about body odors can be dispelled by daily bathing – afterward the healthy odor of sexual arousal will prove pleasant and exciting. A woman should not try to disguise her natural smells or flavors with sprays or deodorants, which can prove intrusive, and anyway, most men find the acid taste of vaginal juices pleasant.

Never get so carried away during sex play that you bite the sex organs. Don't blow into your lover's genitals, since this can be dangerous, and never indulge in oral sex if you have a cold sore or genital infection. It is also a good idea not to indulge in oral sex with a casual partner whose sexual history is unknown to you. There is some evidence that the AIDS virus can be transmitted this way.

PERFORMING CUNNILINGUS

While some men perform cunnilingus because they find it intensely exciting, others may do it more to please their partners. If you are in the latter group, you should never let your partner think that you find it a chore. This is a certain turn-off. Concentrate instead on the sure and certain knowledge that you will give her maximum pleasure. Remember, too, to use your hands to caress her breasts, thighs, and buttocks at the same time to stimulate her further.

If your partner appears to be slightly reluctant, reassure her about how nice you find the experience, especially if you think she is worried about her genitals tasting or smelling bad. You shouldn't have difficulty sympathizing with her if you bear in mind that you have odors and tastes, too.

HOW TO GIVE HER PLEASURE

Women need direct stimulation in order to reach orgasm, so the most important thing that a man can do for his partner sexually is to learn the areas, pressures, and rhythms that excite her most. The clitoris is the most sensitive part of a woman's anatomy and it may easily become exquisitely tender. It is often better in the beginning to direct your attentions to the labia minora and the entrance of the vagina.

Start by kissing and licking her lower belly and the inner side of her thighs, working your way down to her pubic mound. Then, move your tongue over the genital area, flicking it along the fleshy folds up to the clitoris. Thrust your tongue in and out of your partner's vagina to see if she likes it.

Separate the vaginal lips with your hands and then, using your tongue, gently probe her clitoris – first nuzzle and suck it, then vibrate your tongue quickly against it. If given sufficient stimulation, your partner should be able to reach orgasm easily. Once she has climaxed, she will probably prefer not to be stimulated for some time.

It is important to take care with your teeth. Keep them protected by your lips and be careful not to scratch or bite the sex organs, which can be very painful. Make sure, too, that your fingernails are not too long.

Work your way down her abdomen, kissing and licking her skin

PERFORMING FELLATIO

First, find a comfortable position; it is relaxing for your partner if he lies down but you can kneel down in front of him while he stands or sits in a chair. He should always be immaculately clean. You can bathe together or wash him yourself, making this into more foreplay. While you are performing fellatio, caress the rest of his body with your hands to make it really exciting for him.

You can begin by kissing and licking his penis; then, holding the shaft in one hand, swirl your tongue gently around the tip. Stimulate the tip with your tongue and push the tip of your tongue into the slit. Next, explore the shaft, running your tongue around the ridge where it meets the head, and vibrate it gently against the frenulum.

When you feel ready to take his penis into your mouth, cover your teeth with your lips and take in the whole head of the penis. With your teeth well apart, move your mouth up and down, letting your partner guide your rhythm with his hands on your head. Maintain a steady rhythm and firm pressure. Make certain you don't bend the penis too far down when sucking; this can be painful. The penis should always point upward.

Gradually increase your speed until he is about to climax. Then, if you don't want him to ejaculate in your mouth, withdraw and bring him to orgasm with your hand, or switch to intercourse.

As you come to enjoy performing fellatio, you can experiment with some other sensations. Whirl your tongue around the penis while it is deep in your mouth, push it in and out of your mouth, or try sucking on it. The scrotum is fairly sensitive, so you can use your tongue and mouth there as well.

HOW TO PERFORM FELLATIO

1 A woman can stimulate her partner initially by kissing and caressing his abdomen, thighs, and buttocks, as well as the penis and scrotum.

2 Keeping one hand on the penile shaft or scrotum, a woman can use her lips and tongue to stimulate the head of the penis with a variety of movements.

ANAL STIMULATION

For numerous people, the anus and its surrounding area are very sensitive sexually, and for some it is their most erogenous zone. The anal region is well supplied with nerves that follow a similar pathway to the nerves supplying the penis and vagina. Anal stimulation, therefore, gives deep feelings of sexual pleasure unobtainable in other ways, and adds variety to lovemaking. Orgasm that occurs as a result of anal penetration is thought by many to be exceptionally exquisite.

The most basic form of anal stimulation is merely touching your partner's anus during intercourse or oral sex. This is an activity known as "postillionage." More sensation can be produced by inserting a finger into the rectum. When doing this, always lubricate your finger first, and make sure your nail isn't jagged or you could cause harm. Never do this if you have any infection on your finger or hand.

Another technique, gluteal sex, involves the man using the crease of the woman's buttocks as an alternative to the vagina. If the woman contracts her gluteal muscles and rotates her pelvis, the man can thrust into there and reach orgasm this way.

Anal penetration carries with it the risk of AIDS, and if performed over a long time, can lead to stretching of the anal sphincter, which could lead to incontinence. However, the illicit overtones of the act (it is illegal in many parts of the world), the dominant and submissive qualities inherent in it, and the particular sensations it inspires are, to its practitioners, alluring and attractive reasons for indulging in it, and quite a few heterosexuals do.

— STIMULATING A MAN —

The prostate gland and back passage, when stimulated, can provide intense sensations; this technique is particularly useful when a man's virility is flagging. Making certain your finger, or fingers, are well lubricated (lack of a lubricant will be very uncomfortable), insert them approximately 2 inches (5 centimeters) into the rectum. To stimulate the prostate gland, press against the front wall of the rectum with a slight downward pressure. At the same time, apply firm pressure behind the scrotum with the heel of your hand.

— STIMULATING A WOMAN —

Using very gentle pressure, insert a well-lubricated finger into the rectum or move it gently in and out. Keep the heel of your hand pressed firmly between the anus and the vulva. As you apply pressure from the outside, ask your partner to bear down on your finger. This may help to tighten up the anal sphincter deliberately, and then let it relax.

For reasons of hygiene, once you have inserted your finger into the rectum, keep it well away from the vagina, and make sure that you wash it thoroughly immediately afterward.

SEXUAL AIDS

Men and women respond romantically and erotically to environment, ambience, and atmosphere. There is little question that soft lighting, subdued colors, gentle background music, pleasing scents, melodious voices, and soft and sexy clothes all help to reduce inhibitions and increase the possibility of intimacy. There are, however, a variety of other devices and techniques that add to sexual pleasure and which, for some people, may even be a necessity.

VIBRATORS

The first vibrators were fashioned on the dildo, an artificial penis that has been used by both sexes for many thousands of years. The most recent variation on the traditional dildo is the battery-operated vibrator, which

—— MEN AND VIBRATORS ——

It is unlikely that a vibrator will have the explosive effect on a man that it has on a women, although it is able to heighten pleasure enormously in sensitive spots.

The area just behind the root of the penis and in front of the anus is highly sensitive to deep vibration: a vibrator used there will increase sexual pleasure enormously. Almost all of the shaft of the penis, particularly the undersurface, is sensitive to vibration, too, and this rises as the tip is approached. Sensation is exquisite around the frenulum and so arousing when vibration is felt over the tip that a vibrator can sometimes be used as a cure for impotence.

— WOMEN AND VIBRATORS —

A woman who is unable to reach orgasm during intercourse often wonders if there is something physically wrong with her that prevents her from reaching orgasm. A self-induced orgasm answers that question in a few minutes, and it is here that a vibrator may be truly useful. There is certainly nothing wrong with, and virtually no difference between, an orgasm reached with a vibrator and one reached during sexual intercourse. More importantly, a self-induced orgasm gives the emotional and physical foundation for having orgasms during intercourse.

A vibrator, therefore, can tear down the barriers of guilt, shame, and prudery that prevent so many women from finding the sexual fulfilment that they deserve. Some women have for years subconsciously imposed the same kind of paralysis on their sex organs as on their minds. A vibrator provides intense sexual excitement, which is sufficient to overwhelm emotional obstacles, and makes the brain and the genital organs respond explosively in unison.

is widely available in sex shops. Vibrators are used mostly to stimulate a woman's clitoris, and they can be a great help in cases when a woman otherwise has difficulty reaching orgasm during sexual intercourse.

The vibrator works by stimulating the millions of sensory nerve endings in the skin of the woman's labia and the clitoris. A man can also benefit from a vibrator, applying it to his penis and surrounding area to heighten his sensations there.

During intercourse, the penis pushes and pulls against the labia and clitoris and, so to speak, flicks on millions of tiny switches that fire off electric impulses to the brain. In a basic sense, the more sensors the penis stimulates, the greater the sexual sensations. Sad though it may be, a vibrator is better than most penises; in a given moment it can trigger at least a million more sensors than the most educated penis, and that makes orgasm virtually inevitable. This does not mean that a vibrator is necessary, or that the penis is redundant. The whole idea of self-produced orgasm is simply to pave the way for satisfying sexual intercourse.

CREAMS AND LUBRICANTS

The vagina produces a natural lubricating fluid within a few seconds of effective sexual stimulation. This normally makes penetration by the penis easier and pleasurable. However, if a man does not persist with foreplay long enough, the vagina won't be given the chance to produce lubrication. Some women, too, do not produce enough lubricant and most, at different times in their lives, for instance after childbirth and menopause, will produce less secretions than usual. At these times, an artificial lubricant may be used, and creams and jellies that are water-soluble are widely sold. (Take care when using petroleum jelly such as Vaseline®, which may irritate the vagina.)

Creams and lubricants come in handy, too, when anal stimulation or intercourse is contemplated, and when manually stimulating your partner. Many men use them during masturbation to ease friction and enhance their pleasure. During massage, too, scented oils or creams can add to the pleasure.

Many women feel pressured not just by society or their partners but also by their own feelings about the presence or absence of lubrication as a sign of arousal. It is comforting to remember that erection of the clitoris and lubrication of the vagina, even erection of the penis, are merely reflexes that do not always accurately reflect our emotional or aroused state. Women can be intensely aroused without being well lubricated, and similarly men can be intensely aroused without an erection. It is an untenable sexist view of things to think that a well-lubricated vagina is solely an opening for an erect penis.

APHRODISIACS

An aphrodisiac is a drug or substance that increases sexual desire. Despite powerful folklore and considerable effort to find such a substance, no proven, reliable aphrodisiacal drug has ever been found, although a wide variety of chemical products, animal and plant extracts, and foodstuffs have their devotees. Such substances only leave a temporary impression of well-being, which may well be due to the person's faith in them. Spanish Fly or cantharides, if taken internally, causes excruciating irritation to the gastrointestinal and urinary tracts, especially the mucous membranes of the urethra. The resulting irritation can cause death in both sexes.

Pornographic pictures, love potions made from animal parts, opioids, and amulets in phallic form have been used in an attempt to stimulate sexual desire artificially. So far, no universal aphrodisiac has been discovered and, in view of the diversity and complexity of individual tastes, it is highly unlikely that one ever will be. Real aphrodisiacs are the subtle physical and emotional factors that will revive sexual desire when it is low; these include intense love fantasies, erotic dreams, or a particularly attractive quality in a partner.

EROTIC MATERIAL

Reading or watching sexually explicit material can produce genital sensations in both women and men, and can have an effect on sexual behavior. Many men use pornography as an aid to masturbation, and many women find that racy material increases their interest in having sex, although few will admit to it.

If you are open and talk to your partner about your reactions to erotic stimuli, you will discover that you have many areas in common, including things that turn you both on or off. If we can free ourselves from the social customs of the past, the emphasis on the mechanical in early sex books and our own ingrained perspectives, we can find that we are always in a situation to be turned on. It is reassuring to realize that in any situation we can control our sexual response, through our own selection of stimuli, by sharing with our partners and by being aware of the different needs we have for love. In realizing this we liberate ourselves.

If, however, you pressure your partner to watch material she or he finds offensive, or you force your partner to join in sexual activities that she or he doesn't enjoy, then the problems involved go far beyond your sex life. What is at stake is more likely to be whether either of you actually wants to continue in a relationship in which one person's views and preferences are given unequal weight, and whether the other is willing to change his or her attitude.

FANTASIES

Everyone fantasizes. It would be very odd if we didn't, because fantasy is a form of sexual rehearsal along paths that are familiar and also some that are entirely new and imaginary. We all respond to fantasies because the brain is the most important organ of sexual pleasure. As the seat of emotions, it can be responsible for turning us on or off sex. If we are full of resentment, grief-stricken, angry, anxious, or miserable, the most

——— MEN'S FANTASIES ———

- Being involved in group sex.
- Watching others having sex.
- Making love in public.
- Having sex with a woman other than one's regular partner; she can be a celebrity, neighbor, previous lover, or friend.
- Watching two women you know making love together; one could be one's partner, the other a relative, friend or neighbor.
- Being forced by a woman to have sex.
- Forcing a woman to have intercourse against her will.
- Forcing a woman to have oral sex against her will.
- Making love in an unusual place.
- Being part of a threesome with another man and a woman.
- Being part of a threesome with two women.
- Having a homosexual encounter.
- Watching one or more men having sex with other women.
- Being sexually abused by a woman.
- Making love to a virgin.
- Having sex with a woman with enormous breasts.
- Making love outdoors, on a famous monument, for instance.
- Having a woman urinate on you.
- Having a woman use a dildo on you in order to have anal sex.

——— WOMEN'S FANTASIES ———

- Making love with one's partner.
- Making love with a former lover or someone other than one's partner.
- Having sex in an exotic location.
- Being made by a man to have sex against one's will.
- Having sex in public while being watched by others.
- Taking part in group sex.
- Making love with a total stranger.
- Having sex with a partner from a different ethnic group.
- Making love to another woman.
- Being taken from behind by a stranger and never seeing the man's face.
- Stripping in public.
- Sexual activities involving an animal, particularly a horse or dog.
- Watching others having sex.
- Watching your regular partner having sex with another woman, or another man.
- Having a male slave.
- Taking part in a threesome, either with another man or with another woman, and one's usual partner.
- Having sex in unusual and unexpected places or circumstances, for example in a courtroom.
- Working as a prostitute and having a large number of clients to satisfy.
- Being tied down and taken forcibly against your will.

attractive person in the world will not be appealing, and any amount of foreplay will not arouse us. On the other hand, being sexually aware, being interested in sex, thinking about it, and fantasizing about it will all be arousing. In this sense, it would seem that the brain is the most crucial sex organ because it can override our sexual urges in any direction, either by turning them off, or by turning them on. Fantasies, therefore, are one of the cheapest and most effective sexual aids.

The best sexual fantasies, the ones that offer maximum pleasure, usually center around ideal situations – ones that are, for practical purposes, unobtainable in "real life." And, also unlike real life, they can be turned on and off at will, either to accelerate or calm sexual activity. Often, we use fantasy to concentrate our minds on what is actually happening to us during our own lovemaking. We "see" what is happening as well as experiencing it. This helps focus our attention on our own sexual responses, and encourages the brain to respond even more enthusiastically to the signals of arousal it is receiving. It then sends out hormones that increase the excitement in our genital organs.

Many people don't fantasize in terms of stories but in terms of sexual images and, while some people would have difficulty confessing their fantasies, others are willing to discuss a particular set of mental images.

In rare cases, a person can become so fixed on a particular fantasy that they cannot become aroused without it. While a fantasy that exercises such a strong hold over your imagination can be very useful during masturbation, it can get in the way of shared sexual activities. Instead of concentrating on how your partner is reacting, and what you can do to please him or her, you can become fixed on bringing your fantasy to life, and consequently seem remote and nonresponsive.

Sharing fantasies is another way of personalizing your relationship, and can be introduced into a long-term sexual relationship to add new excitement and rekindle arousal. Some people are happy to join in a fantasy once it has been recounted; however, others may find that they cannot cope with the desires expressed, and may take their partner's fantasy as a criticism of their lovemaking, which can put a considerable pressure on the relationship. If you are in doubt about what to share, bide your time until you can see the situation more clearly.

MAKING LOVE

While a large part of being a good lover is to make and keep a relationship exciting, which depends on exploring and mastering a range of sexual activities, to my mind the most important thing is to satisfy each other's emotional needs. Real sexual happiness means having positive feelings about your own sexuality and that of your partner.

Sex is our primary way of showing love. The best sex happens in the best relationships. No one can know instinctively what his or her partner enjoys. Partners should explore and develop their sexuality with honesty and trust: honesty is in itself arousing. Sharing the wonder of sex with a sympathetic, loving, and caring partner can be a magical voyage of intimacy and discovery.

BEING A GOOD LOVER

While a large part of being a good lover is to make and keep a relationship exciting, which depends on exploring and mastering a range of sexual activities, the primary task is surely to satisfy each other's emotional needs. Real sexual happiness is not the direct result of technical ability or athleticism but depends on your having positive feelings about your own sexuality and that of your partner. The best sex happens in the best relationships. True sexual chemistry can develop only when partners are attracted to each other as individuals, not just as representatives of the opposite sex. With affection, honesty, and trust, partners should explore and develop their sexuality together, bearing in mind the likes and dislikes they each have.

A man often forgets that a woman is both sentimental and sensual, so that her idea of lovemaking includes a prologue of emotions tenderly exchanged. In order to recapture these feelings, it helps to look back to the time when you first fell in love with each other, when just sitting together talking or in companionable silence was enough. I'm sure you will agree there was pleasure in every treasured sign of affection – touches, looks, nuzzles, gentle caresses, and kisses. You will have greater pleasure and satisfaction if you remember these earlier emotions when the time comes to arouse one another intensely.

COMMUNICATION IS IMPORTANT

No one can know instinctively what his or her partner enjoys. It is up to each of us to talk about our likes and dislikes; it is not unnecessary, and it is not at all insulting. It is almost impossible to have a good sexual relationship without clear communication.

We should all let our partners know which caresses are pleasurable and which are not. We should always say if something is particularly arousing or painful. Lovers should be bold enough to suggest a different way of making love, and should ask each other questions and make requests. The exchange of these confidences will help build up a better physical relationship, while not doing so may make matters irrevocably worse. This can be achieved by saying that something is pleasant or it is not, making encouraging noises, or moving your partner's hand to a spot where the sensation is more pleasurable.

What is appropriate and enjoyable varies from occasion to occasion, so simply because you have expressed a preference once does not mean that you do not have to express it again, or that you might express a different preference on a different occasion. Good lovers should never take each other for granted.

Ideally when conflicting desires are expressed, or when differing degrees of arousal are experienced, a couple should engage in a process of negotiation. If not, you will find yourselves falling into habitual, routine sexual activities. The best of partners may eventually become bored after years of exactly the same activity in the same sequence, in the same position, in the same bed. Boring sex is rarely rewarding to either partner, and there is a vast range of sexual activities that people find appealing and stimulating. Communication does not mean that everything said has to be negative; say what pleases you, and at the same time listen to what your partner is telling you.

If you want to get more enjoyment out of your sexual relationship, you need a partner's full involvement and participation in lovemaking. For two people to enjoy their sexual relationship fully and completely, both must be able to accept the pleasure a partner gives, and both must be able to enjoy the process of giving a partner pleasure. The most satisfying sexual relationships have the joint commitment and sharing of the two people involved at their heart. The more pleasure you give your partner, the more he or she will want (and need) to give you pleasure in return. A good sexual relationship is always a giving relationship, not a taking one.

TALKING OPENLY ABOUT DESIRES

An amazing number of people find it extremely difficult to talk directly and honestly with their partners about their sexual desires, fears, and problems. Many people have been trained to perceive discussions about sex as being so private, so embarrassing, and so revealing, that they hesitate to talk about their own feelings and wishes even with the person they've been married to for years.

In this context it is absolutely essential for partners to talk to each other about sex, so that their bodies can adjust mutually and their pleasures increase. Despite this, in my experience, most couples never talk to each other about what they do in bed, whether it is good or bad, or whether it gives them any satisfaction. I, for one, find it hard to believe that during the most intense moments of a couple's relationship, neither partner knows what the other is thinking; their minds remain separate whereas their bodies are striving to get as close as two bodies can.

Many women talk freely to their friends about unfulfilled desires, disappointments, and frustrations, but men generally keep their sex lives secret. I'm convinced that there would be far fewer misunderstandings, arguments, and conflicts if both partners would talk openly about their physical and emotional expectations. I believe that nothing but good would come of sharing these innermost desires, however strange and fantastic they might appear to be.

MEN AS LOVERS

Many men, no matter what else they may be, are not skillful lovers. Research has shown that the most consistent complaint made by women is that their partners do not take enough time over foreplay. Most sexual relationships tend to develop on a friendly basis for some time, and then gradually evolve into physical intimacy, stopping at petting. During this time, both partners want to please each other and usually find that they communicate extremely well. This gradual exploration and steady development means that couples are sexually relaxed on the first occasion they try intercourse. But over time, with many men seeing penetration as the goal to be achieved as quickly as possible, talking and foreplay dwindle, much to the universal disappointment of women.

MEETING WOMEN'S NEEDS
What the majority of men don't seem to understand is that during foreplay the progress from kissing and cuddling to caressing the breasts, nipples, and clitoris is not only very exciting and pleasurable for a woman, and incidentally to most men, it is absolutely necessary for a woman's arousal, and crucial to her pleasure and satisfaction. Without it, a woman is not sexually aroused or an uninhibited participant, and is not even physiologically ready. But, worse, after sexual intercourse she is unsatisfied and resentful and remains wide awake while her partner turns over and goes to sleep. Men and women are mismatched in this respect because a man is much more easily and quickly aroused, and reaches orgasm in a very short time in almost any situation. Is it any wonder that sex can end up being a battleground, very often of unspoken resentments and hostilities, and becomes more and more uninteresting and infrequent.

PERFECTING YOUR TECHNIQUE
Some of the things women say about men indicate what they would like to see changed.

"I'd like him to touch me all over a lot more – more foreplay, more heavy petting, more kissing everywhere and more oral sex."

"I love my breasts and nipples to be fondled and caressed, and I've always wondered if I could have a climax just by simply being played with, but my partner is too impatient."

"My partner thinks it's "soft" to kiss." Men should be sensual as well as sexual and many feel uneasy about engaging in purely pleasurable activities. To overcome this, when giving caresses, think of the pleasure you are providing to a loved one. Most women find foreplay hugely enjoyable, and see hugs and kisses as the true signs of affection. Try to find your partner's most sensitive areas and the kind of stimulation she prefers.

Don't be afraid to relax and let your partner take the initiative. Let her know, either in words or gestures, what feels especially good and, if necessary, guide her hand with yours. Try to concentrate on what you feel and the proximity of her body as she touches you. Respond to your feelings by breathing more heavily, moving, or expressing pleasure verbally. Most women find a responsive man very exciting. Don't feel that you have to be successful at every sexual encounter. Most women are quite sympathetic to an occasional failure, and may even view it as an opportunity to show their love.

WOMEN AS LOVERS

While we know that men are easily aroused and reach orgasm more quickly and easily than women, not all are quite as sexually straightforward as many women believe.

MEETING MEN'S NEEDS

I have no doubt that men also require the excitement and gratification derived from an emotional involvement in love-making. There is hardly a man who does not need to feel loved, admired, and physically cherished if he is to experience the true depths of sexual pleasure with his partner. Yet far too many women tend to place the entire responsibility of initiating and orchestrating sex on their men. Traditionally, the man suggests sex and the woman either accepts or rejects him, and in this way the man usually determines how much sex a couple has. This amounts to a great deal of pressure, and many sensitive men do not really relish having such a burden. Better sex and happier couples ensue when partners feel equally free to suggest or refuse sex, and do so equally often.

Taking responsibility for suggesting sex also means that lovemaking will result more from inclination rather than obligation. Women can say "yes" easily to sex but be uninvolved. For a man, a compliant but unresponsive woman will never be as exciting or as satisfying as a woman who is involved and skillful.

PERFECTING YOUR TECHNIQUE

To be a good sexual partner means that you should keep sex interesting, not only by regarding it as the best means of expressing your affection toward your man, but also by experimenting with a variety of techniques and practices. You should always be willing to take the initiative. Men want to feel that they are accepted by their partners, and are worth making an effort to arouse and delight. Try some seduction occasionally; tell your man to lie back and enjoy your caresses as you take the active role.

Remember always to communicate your enjoyment of what you are doing or what is being done to you. Don't be embarrassed about the way you look or sound while making love. Almost all men find expressions of desire and signs of growing sexual excitement in women extremely stimulating. Far too many women give their partners too little feedback so that their men tend to feel discouraged and unappreciated for what they are doing and will, in future, pay less attention to foreplay.

Use your imagination as much as possible. This is especially important in long-term relationships when boredom can easily set in. In addition to picking and choosing among the entire range of the normal sexual repertoire, introduce activities that will bring novelty into your relationship. Suggest taking a bath or shower together; make love outdoors in a private place; plan lunch at home but make love instead; abandon your bed in favor of the floor, sofa, or a rug; use a mirror to watch yourselves making love; view a sexy video together; or indulge in a sexual banquet of both partners' choosing.

Show enthusiasm toward your partner if he suggests ways of enlivening your sex life. Unless something is painful or distressing, it is always worth finding out whether or not it gives you pleasure. In sex, as in all things, let your instincts be your guide.

VARYING EXPERIENCES

Earlier we looked at the individual experiences of men and women in achieving orgasm. But, as with all the best love-play, orgasms should be a shared experience. That doesn't mean to say, however, that they must occur necessarily at the same time.

Some couples feel – erroneously – that orgasm must be simultaneous to be perfect. This is a romantic notion that doesn't necessarily work for all lovers. At the moment of climax, you move to an entirely different level of consciousness, and you become totally absorbed in the experience. If you are prevented from doing so because you need to know where your partner is, you may not be able to manage a climax at all, or not manage it as well. And, for many lovers, watching the other experiencing his or her orgasm is the greatest of sexual turn-ons.

For most couples, the attainment of simultaneous orgasms only happens now and then, and sex is no less enjoyable for that. Seeking simultaneous orgasms should not become obsessive. There are many patterns of successful lovemaking that exclude simultaneous orgasms (and some that exclude all orgasms), but nonetheless draw couples very close and have infinite positive effects on everyday experiences as well as on social and family life.

And then there are the exceptional circumstances – prolonged and multiple orgasms – that are quite rare unless both partners are aware of each other's sexual needs and are generous enough to look after them. Most couples find these forms of sexual intercourse the most exciting and sexually satisfying, but they take quite a lot of practice and are most often found within long-term relationships. Partners must be very familiar with each other and have worked to reach a state of sexual sophistication.

PROLONGED ORGASM

This can be achieved only if a man is able to control his ejaculatory reflex at will. It is a form of sexual union indulged in usually by partners who have been making love together for some time, who know each other well, and who have learned how to adjust to each other's needs. This can be one of the most exciting forms of sexual union, and it is one of the most treasured aspects of a long-term loving relationship.

For it to occur, the woman must be highly aroused during foreplay and then the sexual tension of both partners must be maintained by intermittent thrusting movements, punctuated by pauses from time to time for as long as each partner wishes. When sensation reaches a peak and can't be put off any longer, both partners enjoy orgasm in a mutually agreed, final burst of lovemaking.

MULTIPLE ORGASMS

Until recently, we believed that only women were capable of multiple orgasms, but new research has shown that some men are able to have them, too. Since orgasm is not necessarily synonymous with ejaculation, but is more accurately defined as the intense and diffuse pleasurable sensations the man feels, it is perfectly possible for a man to have several climaxes in fairly quick succession.

—— MAN'S EXPERIENCE ——

American doctors have documented the experiences of multiorgasmic men who had from two to nine orgasms per session. Some ejaculated at the first orgasm, some at the last, and the rest somewhere in between; some even ejaculated more than once. Many of the men first experienced multiple orgasms in middle age.

Probably, more men could become multiorgasmic if they overcame the conditioning that says they will only ejaculate and then detumesce. An un-demanding atmosphere, combined with emotional closeness and the opportunity for leisurely sex, will improve a man's chances of enjoying multiple orgasms, as will having a partner who is sexually responsive and does not easily tire of prolonged intercourse.

However, just as with multiorgasmic women, men who are capable of more than one orgasm will not be able to experience them every time.

To practice becoming multiorgasmic, a man can come to the brink of orgasm while inhibiting ejaculation until he is able to separate the two sensations. In the positive, relaxed atmosphere of a loving relationship, some men will find that they don't necessarily lose their erections, and they will be able to carry on achieving further climaxes.

—— WOMAN'S EXPERIENCE ——

For a woman to enjoy multiple orgasms, her man must exercise careful control to avoid ejaculating, yet give her sufficient deep and rapid thrusting for her to achieve orgasm. Or a woman may use a vibrator, or she or her partner may masturbate her. After each orgasm, both partners rest for a while and then the cycle can begin again. In this way, a woman can enjoy two, three, or many more orgasms. Ideally, her partner will climax simultaneously with her last one, but often the rigid control needed means he experiences his own orgasm only when his partner is fully satisfied.

Most women find that they can build up their level of sexual arousal with practice; the more frequently a woman masturbates, the more pleasure she gets from it, and the more she will want to do so. Most women can improve their chances of multiple orgasm by keeping their pelvic muscles in good condition, and sharing fantasies, but above all, they need to encourage their partners to help them. If you are trying to have multiple orgasms, your partner needs to know; and you should encourage him to carry on stimulating you even after you've had an initial climax. Because a man's experience of orgasm is so different, your partner may think you have had enough of love-play just because he has.

73

POSITIONS FOR MAKING LOVE

Often, when couples whose sex life has gone stale consult me about making improvements, one of the first questions I ask is whether they vary the way they make love. Many of these couples have tied themselves to a single position for lovemaking, and it has simply become boring. The missionary position, with the man on top and the woman underneath, is most commonly used and, for some couples, never varied. (It is so-named because it was forcibly advocated by missionaries who took their faith to "heathen" or "uncivilized" peoples.) For many years the church tolerated this position and no other, since it was thought to be the one in which the woman would almost certainly be fertilized. This rigidly adhered-to tradition allowed the man always to adopt the dominant role during sexual intercourse and to experience most or all of the pleasure of sex.

But between consenting lovers, all coital positions are perfectly normal and legitimate, and everyone's sex lives will certainly be enlivened by a little adventure and experimentation.

CHOOSING A POSITION

There's no such thing as the best position; each couple should experiment and find their own most favorable positions, which will depend on the shape and size of the couple's bodies, both partners' strength and stamina, and any special situations such as a pregnancy, disability, or illness. Couples who are making love and exploring each other for the first time very often experiment with a variety of positions in quick succession in an attempt to satisfy their curiosities.

At the same time, partners should try to find out as much as they can about the other's body so that they can adjust to each other physically. One of the purposes that a book like this serves is to enlighten couples who know little or nothing about loving sex, or who are lacking in imagination, and who cannot believe that there are other positions apart from those they happen to have come across by chance. Remember that expertise can't be attained in a day; it may take months of enjoyable experimentation before a couple finds the several positions that for them are wholly satisfying and fulfilling in every sense.

The following pages illustrate a number of positions. For a variety of reasons, each position has particular benefits for one or both partners. Set out opposite, in no special order, are some of the considerations that each partner in a couple looks for, and that the positions they choose take into account. Both partners should take notice of the preferences of the other, which means that each partner has the responsibility for expressing his or her predilections in the first instance. To enjoy intercourse to the maximum, however, any position in which it is tried should be comfortable and allow freedom of movement, and must accommodate the abilities of the less athletic partner.

Certain positions are uncomfortable or even painful for one partner, some are better for the man than for the woman and vice versa, while others can increase the feeling of pleasure and enhance sexual arousal so that the chances of an orgasm for both partners, but particularly the woman, are increased. This is not to say that any one position is better than another. Each position may have its own advantages in any given situation and on any given occasion, taking account of how each partner feels physically and emotionally.

THE MAN'S CHOICE OF POSITION

• Does it allow good penetration (shallow or deep, as desired)?
• Will he be able to see his partner's vulva clearly?
• Will he have good access to his partner's clitoris?
• Can he reach her breasts with his hands or mouth?
• Can he move easily?
• Will it prolong intercourse or, if desired, is it good for a quick getaway?
• Is it tiring?
• Can his partner move?
• Does it allow for his unusually small or large penis?
• Does it allow full stroke movement?
• If he has erection difficulties, can the position and penetration be achieved without a firm erection?
• Can he kiss his partner and hug and cuddle her?
• Is it good if his partner is much heavier or lighter than he is?
• Does it need a lot of undressing?
• Does it allow him to take the dominant (or passive) role?
• Can he stimulate his partner's buttocks and anal area?
• Is it possible during pregnancy?

THE WOMAN'S CHOICE OF POSITION

• Can she move so that stimulation remains good?
• Does it allow her to see her partner?
• Is it comfortable during the latter stages of pregnancy?
• Can she or her partner reach her clitoris easily?
• Does it allow her to kiss her partner and hold him close?
• Will it stimulate her G-spot?
• Is it comfortable?
• Does it allow her partner to reach her breasts?
• When in the position, can she reach down and touch her partner's scrotum?
• Is it good for cuddling?
• Does it allow good skin contact?
• Is it good for conception?
• What sort of penetration does it allow – shallow or deep – and is it the sort she wants?
• Is it good for learning sex with a new or shy partner?
• Does it stimulate the back or front vaginal wall?
• Does it allow her to take a dominant (or submissive) role?
• Can she look into her partner's eyes and speak to him?

MAN-ON-TOP POSITIONS 1

Man-on-top positions, in particular the "missionary" position, where the man lies between the woman's thighs, are probably the most widely used of all the sexual positions. They give the man almost total control over intercourse, and the woman is allowed very little freedom of movement.

Man-on-top positions (see also p. 78) are particularly good for couples who are just beginning to have sex with each other, since there is full eye contact and the opportunity to communicate with each other so that preferences and responses can be noted. The other advantages these positions offer are plenty of scope for kissing, deep penetration, and manual stimulation, plus access to the male posterior. They are also good if conception is desirable.

2 If the woman brings her leg up to apply pressure to her partner's back, she can control the depth and angle of his thrusts, perhaps so that he presses on the front wall of her vagina, the site of her "G" spot.

1 The man enters his partner straight on so that his penis is parallel to her vaginal walls. If she spreads her legs wide, the stretchy feeling is quite sensuous.

Face-to-face, the couple have full eye contact and can kiss passionately

He can take his weight on his elbows, allowing his partner to move her pelvis more freely

She can use her leg to apply pressure to his back and buttocks, and for some control over his thrusting

3 By bringing up both legs to wrap them around her partner, a fit and supple woman alters the tilt of her pelvis, which can produce pleasing new sensations for both her and her partner, and increases genital contact.

MAN

The man has wide access to his partner for kissing and caressing her upper body and breasts, and he can control his thrusting, speeding up or slowing down as necessary.

WOMAN

Man-on-top positions are very good for kissing and caressing. They also feed a woman's romantic needs. She is being made love to, and can just lie back and enjoy the sensations.

MAN-ON-TOP POSITIONS 2

Man-on-top positions feed a man's need to dominate by allowing him to penetrate his partner deeply, and a woman's desire to be dominated because in them she takes the passive role. Most men enjoy penetrating a woman's body as deeply as possible, and women like it too, especially when they are particularly aroused and want to be "filled up." And, when a woman opens herself completely to her partner, it makes him feel very wanted. In these positions, the man can move freely to control the intensity and depth of his thrusts; the woman can add to his sensations by contracting and relaxing her pelvis to "milk" her partner's penis.

1 As a variation from entering his partner from above, the man can kneel and approach her from a vertical position. He can thus push off against the bed into his partner. She helps increase contact by wrapping her legs around him tightly.

When highly aroused, spreading her legs widely will make deep penetration easier

2 By sliding his partner down the side of the bed, the man can lean forward on her body, taking most of his weight on his forearms while she relaxes and lets herself be taken completely. Movement and penetration are limited so that arousal can be controlled.

MAN

Using these positions the man is able to control his thrusting, and thus the speed at which he achieves orgasm. Control such as this is particularly beneficial if the man is at all worried about losing his erection, or if he wants to delay ejaculation.

WOMAN

Being on her back is relaxing and allows the woman free rein to lie back and enjoy the sensations of being taken or overpowered by her partner. It also "absolves" her from having to be responsible for what happens during sexual intercourse.

3 Finally, pushing them both up the bed, his knees thrusting her legs wide apart, the man can penetrate his partner quite deeply. For her, the sensation is increased by having her knees close to her chest and her bottom raised by a pillow.

Deeply entwined, she feels secure enough to open herself completely to her partner

He uses his thigh and knee to give added pressure to the tempo and depth of his thrusts

WOMAN-ON-TOP POSITIONS 1

Both men and women find the woman-on-top positions extremely satisfying. They enable a woman to take a more active role in controlling both the sensations she gives and those she receives. With her man underneath and relatively immobile, she can stimulate his penis easily by moving up and down, and more readily control the depth of penetration. For the man, such positions prove that his partner is taking the lead; with them, he can feel himself the object of her active seduction. Woman-on-top positions are also comfortable ones, particularly if the woman is much lighter than her partner or if she is pregnant.

He is the passive partner, feeling wanted and seduced, and can concentrate on his own arousal knowing that his partner is controlling her own stimulation

1 To get into the simplest position, where the woman lies on top of her partner with her legs outside, it is probably best to start from a side-on embrace. Then she needs to gently throw a leg across her partner's thighs, and climb gracefully on top. The man, of course, needs to have an erection, which the woman will have to guide inside her.

His hands can caress her back and buttocks, occasionally holding her to guide the angle of penetration

2 If the woman now brings her legs inside her partner's this results in a snugger fit between both genital areas. If she keeps her legs tightly closed, she heightens the friction between the vagina and pelvis. She can add to the sensation by contracting her pelvic muscles.

3 Finally, if the woman spreads her legs out widely to the side, the pubic regions are perfectly aligned. From here, she can press down on her partner's feet, which is highly arousing to him because she is obviously "using" her partner in order to satisfy herself.

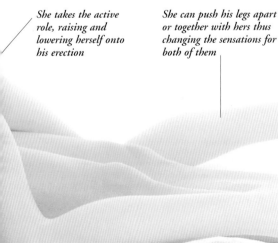

She takes the active role, raising and lowering herself onto his erection

She can push his legs apart or together with hers thus changing the sensations for both of them

MAN
He can lie and enjoy the sensations she arouses. This is useful where he can't take the lead due to fatigue or illness.

WOMAN
In addition to being ideal for a woman to please herself, this helps if a partner is large, or when she is pregnant.

WOMAN-ON-TOP POSITIONS 2

Woman-on-top positions where the woman is sitting up have several advantages. The woman has full view of her man and, by taking all her weight on herself, she can more actively caress him while adjusting his penile movements to her liking. The man is free to fondle his partner's freely moving breasts, which are held tantalizingly close to him, and he can see his penis entering her vagina; both sights are very exciting to him.

1 The woman starts from lying straight on top of her man, straddling his body. She then lifts up her upper body, and gradually brings her legs forward and bends her knees. Initially, to avoid applying painful pressure on her partner, she will put most of her weight on her arms and knees.

She can lean back onto his thighs to take some of her weight from his pelvis

2 By taking all her weight on her knees, she is free to use her hands on her partner – caressing him or holding him down to add an extra element of control, if she so wishes.

MAN

These positions can be very exciting. The man has a full view of both his and his partner's genitals, and good access to her breasts, and he is free to stimulate her and vice versa.

WOMAN

In these positions a woman's breasts and genitals are free to be caressed. In addition, she can readily control the position of her partner's penis and the depth of penetration.

3 Or she can lean back, resting on her arms and hands, taking her legs behind and pressing them close to her partner's body or pushing them away as she chooses. She can even bring her legs forward, stretching them toward her partner's shoulders. In this way, she is free to make swaying or rotating movements.

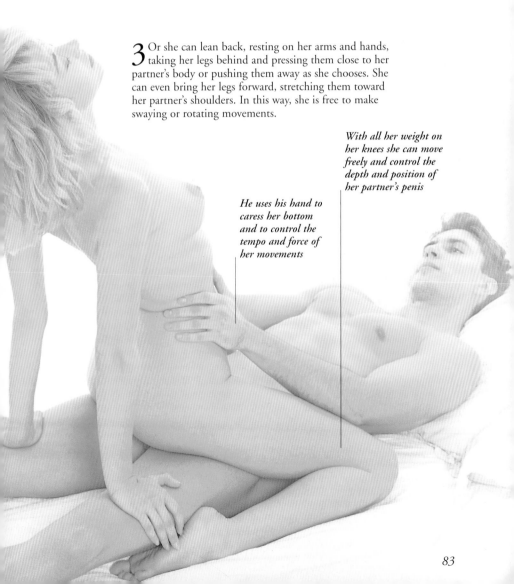

With all her weight on her knees she can move freely and control the depth and position of her partner's penis

He uses his hand to caress her bottom and to control the tempo and force of her movements

STANDING POSITIONS

Making love standing up is most easily achieved when both partners are about the same size. If the man is much larger than his partner, insertion and intercourse are possible only with a certain amount of difficulty and determination. Sexual intercourse standing up can be tiring if it is kept up for any length of time (particularly if there is an uncomfortable difference between the couple's sizes), but owing to the muscular exertion it necessitates, it can considerably increase sexual excitement.

If the man picks up his partner, the greatest amount of exertion is the initial lift. Once he has achieved this, the standing position is not particularly demanding because the weight is evenly distributed between the two partners. From here, making love can continue while standing up, walking, or even dancing.

1 To facilitate insertion, the woman should lift one leg, turn it sideways so that her partner can introduce his penis, and then use both legs for support. The vagina then clasps the penis firmly; she can use her pelvis to make strong sexual movements.

2 Once the man is inside, he can lift his partner by placing his hands under her thighs while she firmly clasps her hands behind his neck and holds onto it. She should then cross her legs behind his back and press her thighs around his hips.

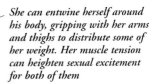

She can entwine herself around his body, gripping with her arms and thighs to distribute some of her weight. Her muscle tension can heighten sexual excitement for both of them

3 If both partners are agile, insertion can be achieved after the woman has been raised off the ground. Now the man can move his partner back and forth with his hands and alter tempo and motion.

MAN

The main benefit of standing positions is the novelty factor, since a degree of agility and strength is required, but they are ideal when the man wishes to dispense with preliminaries. More vigorous thrusting can be achieved if the woman is pressed against a wall or door for extra support.

WOMAN

Standing positions are useful when the time and place for sex is limited, and when she wants to add some variety to her sex life. She can produce a very powerful stimulation on her vaginal lips and clitoris if she leans forward a little and bends her knees while her feet are on the floor.

With his legs bent he can freely thrust into his partner

85

SIDE-BY-SIDE POSITIONS 1

For relaxed, unhurried lovemaking, few positions beat side-by-side ones; it is not at all unusual for couples to fall asleep locked together after making love in this way. When both people are on their sides, rear entry is easy to achieve, and intercourse can be prolonged easily, too, without being too tiring. Such positions also provide maximum body contact and plenty of scope for affectionate caresses.

During pregnancy, and where a man is particularly large, side-by-side positions with the woman facing away are ideal, because he can't put pressure on her this way. These positions also make a relaxing change from more athletic sexual postures.

1 The "spoons" position, with the man cuddling up to the woman's back, is one of the most comfortable and affectionate of all sexual positions. If the woman draws her knees upward, when her partner tucks up against her he can penetrate very easily.

Surrounding her body with his own, he can lovingly kiss and caress her back and neck, and reach around to stimulate her breasts and clitoris

2 Moving onto her back a bit more and raising her bottom slightly lets the woman's partner thrust into her without restriction while having access to her breasts and vagina. There is a lot of skin contact, and the couple can kiss easily and passionately.

Facing variation
This can be achieved from a man-on-top position, without disturbance, if both partners slide onto their sides. Or, it can be initiated this way if the woman lifts or bends her leg to allow the man to insert his penis.

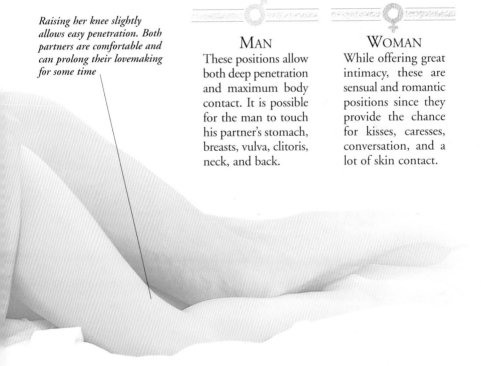

Raising her knee slightly allows easy penetration. Both partners are comfortable and can prolong their lovemaking for some time

MAN
These positions allow both deep penetration and maximum body contact. It is possible for the man to touch his partner's stomach, breasts, vulva, clitoris, neck, and back.

WOMAN
While offering great intimacy, these are sensual and romantic positions since they provide the chance for kisses, caresses, conversation, and a lot of skin contact.

SIDE-BY-SIDE POSITIONS 2

By slight alterations in movement, side-by-side positions can produce a wide variety of new sensations. By rolling backward a woman opens up her vulva considerably and leaves her clitoris free for herself or her partner to caress. Drawing her legs upward increases penetration. By changing the position of his legs and thighs, the man can achieve different movements and control the pressure that the root of the penis directs against his partner's vulva.

Drawing her legs up along her partner's back and sides can increase penetration, particularly if she presses with her legs and feet, coaxing him to thrust farther into her

1 The woman places her bent leg on top of her partner's hip as he pushes his thigh between hers. Then she should lie back and her partner can lean into her, keeping his legs stretched out straight. One of his hands is free to caress her, while she has both free to attend to him. He has more freedom to attempt some active movements while bestowing some caresses.

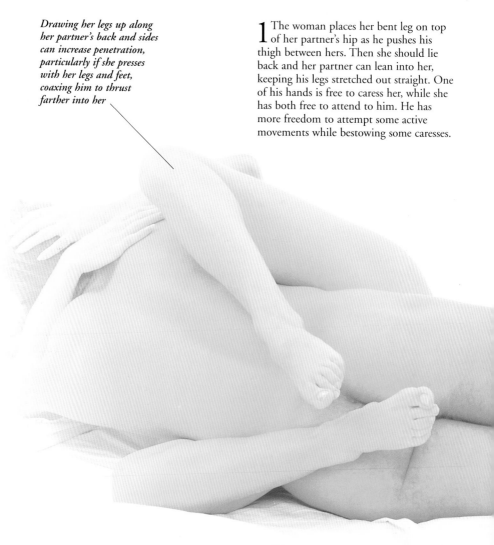

MAN

These positions provide plenty of body contact. The man has enough freedom to experiment with various movements to give new sensations. Movement is somewhat limited, but he is free to grasp his partner's buttocks and pull her onto his penis.

WOMAN

These positions can supply plenty of pressure to the vulva for increased stimulation. They also are good in late pregnancy because they allow a woman plenty of space from her partner, and his penetrating and thrusting can be restricted.

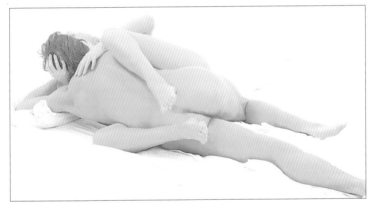

2 By bringing his leg back up, the man can now make strong pushing movements. He can increase the pressure by using his hands to press his partner's buttocks next to his hips.

Changing the position of his legs and thighs can enable him to achieve different thrusting movements and new sensations for them both

REAR-ENTRY POSITIONS

Although not as popular or as romantic as face-to-face positions, couples who have frequent intercourse enjoy the variety that a change to a rear-entry position can bring. Rear-entry positions provide the man with considerable freedom to thrust, and with them he can alter most easily the angle and amount of penile movements. For those women who are fortunate enough to have sensitive "G" spots, these positions result in the greatest stimulation; for those who don't, the different sensations produced can still be extremely exciting.

1 Probably the best known rear-entry position, this is known colloquially as the "doggie." The woman kneels on her hands and knees on the bed or floor, and her partner kneels behind.

2 The vagina is presented directly to the man pressed against her, and she is free to move the angle of her pelvis to give various sensations to both. She can also sway back and forth on her hands and knees.

This position can be very exciting for a lithe woman because excitement mounts from her partner's penis rubbing against new areas of her vagina not normally stimulated

Attempting rear entry is highly stimulating for him since the sensation of dominance is very high

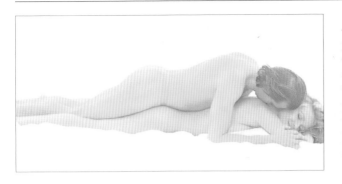

4 If she lies flat and presses her legs together, the woman's clitoris and inner lips will be stimulated indirectly, maintaining her pleasure, and her partner can remain inside, moving how and when he pleases to rekindle desire.

3 The woman will find it more restful to slide down gently onto her stomach and chest while the man takes most of his weight on his arms and hands. (The position can also be initiated in this way.) Deeper penetration will be achieved if she raises her bottom off the bed.

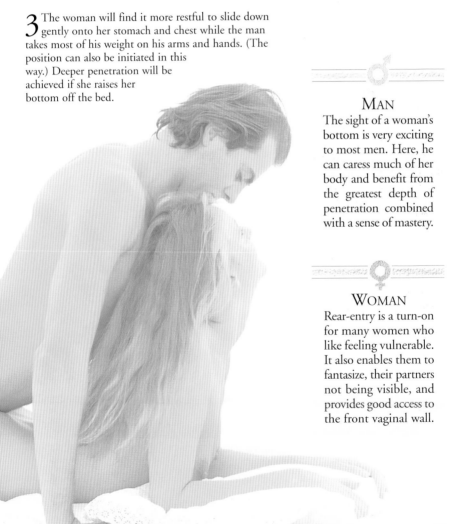

MAN
The sight of a woman's bottom is very exciting to most men. Here, he can caress much of her body and benefit from the greatest depth of penetration combined with a sense of mastery.

WOMAN
Rear-entry is a turn-on for many women who like feeling vulnerable. It also enables them to fantasize, their partners not being visible, and provides good access to the front vaginal wall.

AFTERPLAY

On all levels – physical, emotional, and mental – men and women experience the period of resolution in different ways. While both feel relaxed, calm, and satisfied, having experienced a type of communion that is ecstatic and timeless, a man returns to the normal world and becomes aware of his surroundings much more quickly than a woman does. Detumescence is very fast; the penis becomes flaccid within a minute. A woman takes much longer to surface from the depths of her orgasm, especially if her experience was intense. The engorgement of her genital organs resolves much more slowly, and so do her emotions.

Most women wish to stay in an embrace while their partners wish to get up or simply drift off to sleep. This is a classic instance of why it is important for partners to talk about their desires and to reach a happy solution. If they don't, in time the situation could well lead to unhappiness, frustration, and resentment.

MAN'S EXPERIENCE

Once a man has ejaculated, his interest in sex, and possibly his partner, declines rapidly. His penis will shrink and his sex drive diminishes. For a period of time, depending mainly on his age and health, he can't achieve another erection and so his interest in sex is reduced.

For many men, the penis becomes exquisitely sensitive immediately after orgasm, necessitating instant withdrawal from the vagina. Such men will often withdraw physically from their partners, moving and turning away from them.

In addition, many men are frequently overcome by postcoital somnolence. During the arousal period, a substantial amount of blood flows into the man's pelvic area, and his muscles contract and tighten. This blood is rapidly diverted away from the area after sex, and his muscles relax so that the excitement is replaced by drowsiness and a general feeling of lethargy – something not experienced by the majority of women. A man will often roll over to his side of the bed and go to sleep, leaving his partner in the "damp spot."

Accommodating a partner Most men are totally unaware of how a woman interprets these movements, since she experiences very different feelings after orgasm (see right).

Even if a man is not able to combat his physiological reactions to orgasm, he can and should be sensitive to his partner's emotional needs. A last cuddle and goodnight kiss can be bestowed before he drifts off without too much effort, and it will make all the difference to the woman. A change to lovemaking during the morning, when both partners are fresher, or during the day, may help stave off sleep.

WOMAN'S EXPERIENCE

During the slow phase of detumescence, while still savoring the effects of an orgasm, most women feel a strong desire to remain entwined in their partners' arms, and to lie quietly close to them enjoying nonpassionate embraces and caresses. Some even will wish to lie with their partners' penises still inside them, flaccid though they may be.

There is a theory that a woman's instinct for sexual pleasure is so deeply ingrained in her nature that she has an overwhelming need to maintain body contact with her partner after orgasm, and thereby extend the period of enchantment for as long as possible.

But if her partner gets up or simply rolls over and goes to sleep, a women usually feels neglected and bereft, and this kind of turning off without explanation after sexual union usually leaves her feeling lonely. A sudden withdrawal of this kind seems uncaring, if not brutal, to her.

Prolonging a man's interest A man's usual physiological response to orgasm is one of drowsiness and lethargy, and this is enhanced if lovemaking is left to times when he is already feeling tired and ready for sleep. Therefore, a change to morning lovemaking may bring about a more affectionate afterplay.

To encourage your man to stay awake, keep conversation light and romantic; tell him how much you love him and how wonderful he is. It is a good idea to avoid discussing household problems, which is certain to send him off to sleep. Make sure, too, that after having sex it is not you who rushes off immediately to get washed. If you must clean yourself, suggest you have a bath together.

INDEX

ACKNOWLEDGMENTS

The publisher would like to thank the following individuals and partnership for their contribution to this book.

PHOTOGRAPHY
All photographs by Paul Robinson

ILLUSTRATIONS
Kuo Kang Chen, Sue Linney

ADDITIONAL EDITORIAL ASSISTANCE
Claire Cross, Maureen Rissik, Iris Rosoff

INDEX
Hilary Bird

TEXT FILM
The Brightside Partnership, London